W9-CZZ-431

**Mr. John McFarland**
172 Pleasant Valley Rd.
Rainbow City, AL  35906-8202

# AMERICAN
# GLASS

Courtesy of the Metropolitan Museum of Art

SALT CELLAR    CREAM JUG

AMERICAN EIGHTEENTH CENTURY

# AMERICAN GLASS

*By*

MARY HARROD NORTHEND

*Illustrated with Photographs from
the Collection of the Author*

TUDOR PUBLISHING CO.
NEW YORK

Copyright, 1926,
By DODD, MEAD AND COMPANY, Inc.

NEW EDITION NOVEMBER, 1935
SECOND PRINTING JANUARY, 1936
THIRD PRINTING MARCH, 1936
FOURTH PRINTING JANUARY, 1937.
FIFTH PRINTING JANUARY, 1939
SIXTH PRINTING OCTOBER, 1940

MANUFACTURED IN THE UNITED STATES OF AMERICA BY
MONTAUK BOOKBINDING CORPORATION

I DEDICATE THIS BOOK
TO
MARY J. ALLEN

# PREFACE

THE history of American Glass is most confusing, especially that which was made during Pioneer days, when little consideration was given to preserving records; yet by gleaning here a fact, there another, we are enabled to piece together an authentic story. Through its telling one learns how many stumbling blocks lay along its progress, until one wonders how our forefathers had the courage to keep on until success was assured.

Each attempt brought us nearer to the end, a bit farther along the paths that led us on and on, and it is only by comparing the work of yesterday with that of to-day that we fully realize the great stride that has been made, bringing us to an equal footing with other glass-making countries who have spent centuries in making productions before we as a nation entered the field.

The story of glass is in reality one that has never been fully told, but it has been my endeavor to keep close to the spirit of the times so that he who reads may learn of its evolution which finally ended in acknowledged success.

This task has been materially lightened by those who through many years have made a thorough study of this

# Preface

industry and who have willingly given to me facts which have aided in filling in gaps not understood before. Many untold facts concerning the inner life of the oldest Glass Manufactory still in existence, The Owen Bottle Works, Toledo, have been related to me by Mr. William S. Walbridge, brother-in-law of the late owner. Mr. Stephen Van Rensselaer of Peterborough, N. H., Mr. Frederick Carder of the Corning Glass Works, Martha Kingsbury Colby and others have given their much appreciated advice and valuable information.

To Miss Josephine Lovell of New York is given thanks and credit for revising and editing this work.

# INTRODUCTION

GLASS in its everyday dress is so commonplace with us that we rarely stop to think of the romance inseparably linked with its history. Nor do we often consider what life might be without this truly marvelous substance which makes possible light and sun in our homes, which gives us dishes for our tables, lenses for our telescopes and microscopes, and insulation for our electric fixtures; which is indeed the servant of art, science and general utilities.

Its beginnings are shrouded in mystery, so far away that no man knows who discovered the first crude process, and, as in all such mist-hung origins, myth and fable play their part.

One of the traditions is that it was the product of divine wrath, having occurred when fire from heaven vitrified the bricks which too ambitious mortals were using to build the Tower of Babel.

Another story, often quoted from Pliny, is that a company of Phœnician sailors, returning from Egypt to Syria with a cargo of natron, or soda, were driven ashore by a storm at the mouth of the river Belus. Here they

[ ix ]

made a fire of seaweed on the beach to cook their meal
and rested their pots on blocks of the natron. When the
fire went out they discovered that its heat had melted the
natron and the sand, which, together with the ashes of
the seaweed, had formed the first glass ever made by man.

Practical glass makers refuse to believe this story, although they admit that the ingredients of glass were
present. They say that a heat of at least 1800 degrees
Fahrenheit is needed to fuse the materials of which glass
is made, and that such a temperature could not be produced by a small fire in the open in the ordinary course
of cooking a meal. However, Alexander Nesbitt, in his
book on the subject, points out that glass is sometimes
produced accidentally in metallurgical processes, and occasionally when vegetable substances containing both
silica and an alkali (such as reeds and straw) are burned
in large quantities; and he suggests that such an accident
might easily have occurred in Egypt, where huge masses
of straw are frequently piled up.

In any case, all the facts available point to Egypt as
the original source of this beautiful, versatile and exceedingly temperamental substance. Some of the most ancient
tombs of that ancient land have yielded glass objects,
and in the tomb of Beni Hassan, near Thebes, wall paint-
ings were found clearly depicting men occupied in blowing glass, by practically the same methods and with much

the same tools as those used in the making of fine glassware at the present time.

There is perhaps no branch of collecting in which the terms are less standardized than in glass, where even the initiated amateur often uses words in a broader or more limited application than the professional glass worker. Therefore, something more than a surface acquaintance with these terms will help to make the collecting of American glass a pleasure to the intellect as well as to the artistic sense; and there is no better way of clearing up the haziness that often surrounds such terms as "Crown," "Flint," or "Three Mold," than by acquiring at least a casual knowledge of the history of glass, its ingredients, and the processes of its manufacture.

To go into it fully would be the work of a lifetime, and would lead to a series of volumes that would dwarf the most complete encyclopedia ever published. I am not, of course, going to attempt anything so ambitious. However, since America, in the making of glass as in most other things, is truly "the heir of all the ages," some knowledge of the industry before its introduction into this country is almost essential to an understanding of the place held by American glass as well as of the terms applied to the many shapes, varieties, and qualities that are of interest to the collector.

The life story of glass naturally falls into two divi-

# Introduction

sions, one having to do with its ornamental use, and the other with its development as an industrial asset. It is in this second phase that it has made the greatest progress recently, and it is to our own country that we must turn for the most significant achievements in that channel of its development.

From the small glass objects found in the tombs of the Pharaohs to the plate glass window of the twentieth century is a long journey, but a thrilling one, and it is the purpose of this book to mark some of the milestones on that trail.

# TABLE OF CONTENTS

[ xiii ]

# ILLUSTRATIONS

# Illustrations

# THE FORERUNNERS OF
# AMERICAN GLASS

# Chapter One

IT seems certain that in its infancy glass was an aristocrat, and its progress to the state of ubiquity which it occupies in this democratic age has been one of gradual and slow evolution. Since early documents on the industry are almost entirely lacking, we can only build up by conjecture a picture of the esteem in which it was held in its first days, thousands of years ago, when it was classed as a fit associate of the gems made in Nature's own workshop.

Among the Egyptians it was considered valuable enough to deck a Pharaoh, and in the tomb of Tut-Ankh-Amen, so lately excavated, one of the treasures found was the Collar of Nekhebet. This is described as "composed of two hundred and fifty-five separate gold plaques, inlaid in cloisonné fashion with jasper, lapis lazuli and turquoise-colored glass." This use of it in the burial of a monarch seems fairly good evidence that it was not made as a spurious thing, intended to deceive those who could not afford real turquoise, but that it possessed an intrinsic value due to the difficulty and expense of manufacture.

Within a restricted range these early workers in glass did remarkable things. In "Elements of Glass," a book for practical glass makers, written by Benjamin Franklin Biser, a high testimonial to their skill appears:

"The invention and ingenuity of the ancients," Mr. Biser writes, "was most remarkable in producing variety in glass, devising means of decoration and methods of manipulation. Many processes now in vogue, which are supposed to be recent discoveries, have in reality been anticipated by the ancients. To demonstrate this: Among the relics taken from the tombs of Thebes are specimens of glass coins with hieroglyphical characters which prove that the Egyptians must have been acquainted with the art of pressing glass, while hot, into metallic molds. This has always been considered a modern invention. The Egyptians pressed glass into figures of deities, sacred emblems adapted for mosaic work; colored it to imitate precious stones; worked it into beads and necklaces; and used clay and wire molds with which to form cups, vases, etc. . . . Their ingenuity, which devised so many modes of ornamentation, so many shades of color—primitive tools and impure materials considered—demands our unbounded admiration. Circumstances seem to demonstrate that the industry was carried on by many artificers, each working on a small scale."

From the scene of its invention or discovery the art of glass making spread gradually and slowly among the civilized nations, and Rome became the leader in the work, holding her supremacy until the descent of the Northern Barbarians in the fifth century all but destroyed this and every other art of the Western World.

Throughout the Dark Ages that followed, until the dawn of the Renaissance, the art of glass making seems to have survived in Europe only, or at least principally, as a branch of the Church's handiwork, where it was made in small quantities for use in mosaics and windows to embellish sacred buildings.

Just how the industry reached Venice is more or less a matter of speculation. Some writers tell us that the secrets of glass making were kept alive in the Orient and were carried back to Venice by merchants from that city who maintained trade with Eastern points even during the Dark Ages. Others say that when Rome was sacked some of the glass workers of that city sought refuge in Venice and kept the art alive there throughout the centuries. Probably there is some truth in each of these accounts.

In any event, about the end of the eleventh century, Venetian glass began to be mentioned by contemporary writers, and by the thirteenth century the "Bride of the Adriatic" was famous as the source of beautiful glass. In 1291 glass houses had become so numerous that they were regarded as a fire menace, and laws were passed forbidding furnaces within the city. As a result of this legislation the glass makers were concentrated on the island of Murano, just outside the city limits; and it was from this island that the art of glass making spread throughout Europe and eventually found its way to this Western Continent, the very existence of which was undreamed of by the first glass makers of Murano.

The period of Venetian glass was in many respects the golden age of glass making, as well as the golden age of the glass maker, provided he could accept honors and riches as a just exchange for personal liberty; for that was the choice he had to make. So jealous of their supremacy in glass making were the members of the Venetian Council that they made it a crime, punishable by death, for a glass maker to leave Murano or to impart the secrets of glass making to any foreigner.

To offset these restrictions, they conferred upon all glass workers the title "gentleman," which was in that day not an idle word but in reality a patent of gentility. One evidence of this was that a nobleman of Venice might, if he chose, marry the daughter of a glass maker without jeopardizing his nobility; though if he should so far forget himself as to marry the daughter of a man who earned his living in any other line requiring manual labor he would forfeit his right to associate on equal terms with the scions of other noble families.

In the days of Venetian supremacy blowing was the only method commonly used in shaping glass, and the "metal" was of a kind that lent itself better to delicacy of manipulation than to external finishing, such as cutting or etching. Therefore, Venetian glass is marked by a delicacy and fragility of appearance that sets it apart from all other types.

In spite of the penalties risked by their acts, glass makers did from time to time leave Murano and go into other countries, and in this way the secrets of Venetian glass were gradually spread throughout Europe. Germany, France, and the Low Countries developed excellences of their own, which later were brought over to the new world by pioneer glass workers.

England lagged behind the Continent somewhat, but during the reign of Elizabeth a definite beginning was made, and a new era in glass making was introduced through the perfecting of a kind of glass known as flint. Lead was the new ingredient that gave this glass its distinctive characteristics, great brilliancy and a comparative softness that made it easy to cut or etch the surface.

This was the state of the art of glass making at the time when America began to look toward the old world for instructors and workmen to develop the industry in the crude settlements of the new continent.

# EARLY GLASS MAKING IN
# AMERICA

## Chapter Two

LEAVING behind us the glamour of Old World Glass, glass marvelous in color, exquisite in design, intriguing in decoration, we cross tempestuous seas to study at first hand the progress of glass making in America.

Over four centuries have gone by since that twelfth of October, 1492, when Christopher Columbus, seeking the East Indies, discovered a new land. Acrimonious contentions arose in England concerning the authenticity of his reports and the advantage of sending colonists to make homes for themselves in what was then only a vast wilderness. Not until a book by Captain John Smith was published in 1605, setting forth the advantages of the new-found land, was interest in England thoroughly awakened.

This was during the period of the Pagan Renaissance when King James First was seated on the throne, an ambitious monarch who was quick to realize the possibilities not only of enlarging English territory, but also of obtaining much wealth through founding a plantation on Virginian shores. In consequence he issued a decree authorizing the London Company to occupy the tract of land lying between the 34th and 38th degrees of latitude, known to-day as North Carolina and Virginia, and to gather a group of honest, responsible men and send them to found a colony.

Early in the winter of 1606 a fleet of three small vessels, under Captain Christopher Newport, sailed from London with one hundred and sixty souls, "adventurers and mariners," and after four months on the ocean, sailing by way of the West Indies, the journey ended when they sighted the coast of what is now known as Chesapeake Bay.

They followed its shores until they reached a winding river which they named the *James* in honor of their sovereign. On the shores an elevated neck of land, covered by forests, extended far out into the river. Undaunted, the planters landed, and picking their way along an Indian trail, which led ultimately to the crest of the hill, they found a sightly spot on which they decided to settle. This, too, they called in honor of their king, *Jamestown*.

Soon the sound of the adze rang out cheerily in the woodlands as the monarchs which had stood like sentinels over the Indians for centuries were laid low, to be later cut into slabs to serve the needs of an alien people. First they built a fort, triangular in outline, and strengthened by an outer palisade, and within the protection of this rude structure they made "a settled street of houses, running along so as each line of the angle had its street."

These "houses" were mere cabins, constructed from green slabs which shrank as they dried out, and left great cracks in the walls.

It is evidence of the important part that glass already played in the domestic arrangements of the people, that one of the first things the colonists asked to have sent was a supply of this commodity. Apparently the London Company, realizing the difficulties of transporting so fragile a material, decided that it would be better to provide the colony with the means of making its own; for the second supply, which reached Jamestown in October, 1608, brought over eight "skillful workmen from foreign parts," Dutchmen and Poles, to teach the colonists how to make glass, tar, pitch and soap ashes.

Within a short time a glass house was set up in the woods on the other side of the isthmus, about half a mile from the town. This is the first industry recorded as being established in what is now known as the United States of America.

It seems to us a mystery that the settlers, realizing the dangers of an isolated building, should have gone into the heart of the forest to build not only the glass house but also houses for the workers to live in. Perhaps it was some such fear of fire as caused the Venetian Council to concentrate the glass workers of that city on the island of Murano.

Whatever the reason, the glass house was built at a distance from the fort and the records that remain tell of skirmishes with the Indians in the vicinity of the building, one of them being a hand to hand encounter between Captain John Smith and Wochinchopunck, the chief of the Paspabeghs.

What the "skillful workmen from foreign parts" were able to accomplish in the way of glass making is not recorded, and the question of their fate is one that history leaves unanswered. Perhaps they succumbed to the Indians; perhaps they wearied of pioneer life and went back to their native lands. In any case the glass house fell into disuse for some years until, in 1621, the London Company contracted with Captain William Norton to take to Virginia four Italians and two servants, with their wives and children. Upon arrival Captain Norton was to set up a glass furnace and make glass of all kinds, including beads for traffic with the Indians. By the terms of his contract he was to have the exclusive right to make glass in the colony for seven years and was to share in the profits equally with the company.

Just how great a variety of glass was made under this contract we do not know. Beads seem to have been the most profitable articles, and these were made in great quantities. The Indians, attracted by the bright colors of the baubles, eagerly exchanged valuable pelts for

A DISPLAY OF MRS. ANNIE E. LIBBY'S COLONIAL
GLASS AT NEWTON CENTRE, MASS.

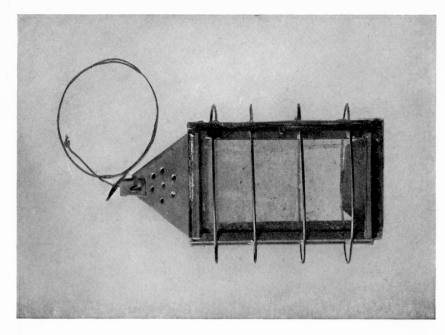

OLD SHIP LANTERN

OLD SHIP LANTERN, PROBABLY
EARLY AMERICAN GLASS

necklaces which they proudly wore dangling upon their breasts as they donned their war paint. So popular with the native tribes were these necklaces, and so far-reaching was the news of this venture, that Indians came long distances through the forest in the hope of securing even a single string.

We know something of the character of these beads, for a handful is treasured in Memorial Hall at Fairmont Park, Philadelphia; a mere dozen to be sure, but sufficient to show that they were made in a variety of shapes and colors.

The workmen, being Italians, perhaps Venetians, naturally knew the value of color and variety of form in beads; and they made them to suit the demand, for gorgeous decoration was what the Red Men sought. Some of these beads were no larger than a pea, red in coloring, and contrasted most effectively with others melon shaped, of opaque white, decorated with grooved lines of light green. Others were in shades of blue, turquoise and darker, some of them as somber as a midnight sky and giving one the impression that they had been buried long centuries ago.

Possibly other things were made, but if they were we have no specimens to show what manner of glass was produced. Captain Norton died a year or two after landing, and George Sandys, the treasurer of the colony, took his place as manager of the glass house. We know that he found the work disappointing, partly due to the difficulty of securing the proper kind of sand and partly because of trouble with the Italian workers, who were discontented and homesick, and the glass house gradually fell into disuse.

After these attempts, glass was made here and there, but during the century following the Jamestown experiments no plant lasted long.

One of the noteworthy enterprises within this period was in Salem, Massachusetts. In 1639, a glass house was erected here of such size that, together with the adjoining buildings, it covered thirty acres of land. The plant was located in that part of the city which now borders Aborn Street. Authentic records are in existence in the First Church of Salem, where one finds the following entry: "graunted to the glass makers severall acres of ground adjoining their houses, one acre to Ananias Conklin, two acres apiece to the other two, viz.; Lawrence Southlick and Obadiah Hullme."

The General Court, realizing that this plant was of consequence, authorized the town to lend to the proprietors the sum of thirty pounds, "to be repaid when they are able to do so." Whether they were ever able to repay the loan is not on record, but some years later the industry was still struggling for existence; and, though it has been dead these many years, it is claimed that pieces of the original glass have been dug up in the vicinity of the original works quite recently.

Others of the early glass making establishments were in New Amsterdam, where Jan Smeedes and Evert Duyckinck, two honest Dutch burghers, had their shops in what is now William Street, then known as Glass Makers Street.

In his "Reminiscences of Glass Making," written in 1850, Deming Jarves recorded that "The Historical Society of Brooklyn, N. Y., has in their cabinet 'a glass bottle, the first one manufactured at a glass-works started, in 1754, near the site of the present glass-works in State Street. This enterprise, we are informed, was brought to an untimely end for want of sand—that is, the right kind of sand.' From this we infer it must be a flint-glass bottle, as the sand suitable for green or black glass abounds on their shore."

For years this bottle figured in the literature of American glass, and quite a wealth of legend grew up around it, passed on from person to person, none of whom had seen it. Finally, Frederick William Hunter, driven by the spirit of research to which we owe his great work on Stiegel, made a determined effort to look upon this treasure, only to find that if there had ever been such a bottle it had long ago vanished and left no trace.

There were many reasons for the failures that ended the succession of short lived efforts in glass making in the early days of this country. For one thing transportation, both of raw materials and of manufactured glass, was a difficult problem.

Even when roads had replaced Indian trails, the business could not be carried on at a profit; for the roads were rutty, the wagons springless, and, especially in the spring of the year when the frost had come out of the ground, there was much breakage. Glass making more than any other industry is dependent on safe and easy transportation, particularly in a land of great distances like this, where economy requires that the factory shall be located near the fuel supplies on which the industry is so dependent, and these are, or at least were in those early days, likely to be some distance from the settled sections where a market is to be found.

Moreover, few of the early glass makers had any government protection, such as Norton had in his contract calling for seven years' exclusive privilege; while the glass makers of most of the European nations were given very considerable benefits by their governments. As a result it was possible for the colonists to buy imported glass of fine make at prices that compared favorably with those charged by the native manufacturers for the necessarily cruder articles they produced.

# Early Glass Making in America

As the land became more thickly settled, an abundance of sand glass was discovered in various parts of the country. The lack of skilled workmen and the long time required to train them for the industry presented a serious obstacle. But our ancestors were men of strong will; otherwise they could never have laid the foundation of the country. In the field of glass making, as in many others, they were unwilling to yield to defeat, realizing the value of glass to a fast developing country. So from time to time foreign glass makers were brought over and the work went on, the ventures rising and falling like the tide until the close of the Revolutionary War, when it became a settled industry and began to progress along the rising path that has led to the present secure place held by America in this field.

# THE WISTARS AND SOUTH
# JERSEY GLASS

## Chapter Three

IT was in 1739 that the making of glass in America may be said to have begun in earnest. By an agreement dated December 7th, 1738, Caspar Wistar, "brass button worker," of Philadelphia, contracted with Captain John Marshall to bring over with him on his next voyage from Rotterdam four "experts in glass making," John William Wentzell, Caspar Halter, John Martin Halton and Simon Kreismeier. The terms of the contract were that these experts should teach glass making to Caspar Wistar and his son, Richard, and to no one else; and in exchange Caspar Wistar was to provide land, servants, food, and materials for a glass factory in the Province of New Jersey. He was also to advance money for all expenses, including their support, and was to give them one-third of the net profits.

The place selected for the venture was in South Jersey, near the village of Allowaystown, Salem County, and the little settlement was christened Wistarberg. The buildings were erected during the fall and summer of 1739 and before the end of the year production was begun.

To us who are now garnering with eager hands each piece of glass that can by any stretch of the imagination be ascribed to the Wistarberg works, it is difficult to realize that this was merely one of the business ventures of the day, evidently not known far beyond the vicinity of its operations, and not even recognized as a leader by glass makers of the succeeding period. In his "Reminiscences of Glass Making," written a century later, Deming Jarves credits Robert Hewes, "a well-known citizen of Boston," with being the first who made an attempt to establish a window-glass manufactory on this continent. This attempt was made, Mr. Jarves writes, "shortly after the close of the Revolutionary struggle, we think about the year 1785." Yet in 1769 Richard Wistar advertised in the *Pennsylvania Gazette* as follows:

"Made at subscribers Glass Works between 300 and 400 boxes of Window Glass consisting of common sizes, 10x17, 9x11, 8x10, 7x9, 6x8. Lamp glasses or any uncommon sizes under 16x18 are cut on short notice. Most sort of bottles, gallon, ½ gallon, quart, full measure ½ gallon cafe bottles, snuff and mustard bottles, also electrofying globes and tubes, etc."

That the "made in America" slogan is not so recent as we have been led to think, and that the early business men were fairly well trained in the modern theory that an advertisement ought to arouse interest in more than one of the advertiser's products, is evidenced by Mr. Wistar's conclusion:

[ 24 ]

# Wistars and South Jersey Glass

"All glass American Manufacture, and America ought also encourage her own manufacture. **N. B.** He also continues to make the Philadelphia brass buttons, noted for their strength, and such as were made by his deceased father and warranted for 7 years.

"RICHARD WISTAR."

However, the question of priority in the making of window glass is not one that gives us much concern. The products of the Wistar works that interest us are the "most sort of bottles," and more especially, the things that Richard omitted to advertise—the bowls, the pitchers and the vases, the scent bottles, and the drinking glasses that went out for fifty years to the homes of those patriotic Americans who did encourage American manufacture.

If only these early craftsmen had had a little more training in modern methods of publicity they might have made it an easier matter for the collector of to-day to identify their wares. The possessor of a beautiful old bowl who could turn it upside down and show the name "Wistar" impressed on the glass while still in a plastic state could snap his, or her, fingers at the doubting Thomas who questioned its authenticity—provided, of course, he could prove that the trademark was not an imitation!

The practice of marking glass was not unknown to

these manufacturers. Edwin A. Barber, in his book, "American Glass, Old and New," mentioned a drinking glass which he had seen in the possession of General Isaac J. Wistar of Philadelphia. This was one of a dozen, made for the founder of the works, which had been distributed among his descendants and had come down by well-authenticated descent. On one side of this glass was the etched monogram of Caspar Wistar and on the other a full length figure of a deer with branching antlers.

However, probably much of the zest of collecting glass would be gone if the matter were as easy as this, for part of the pleasure an expert gets out of the pursuit is the developing of that subtle sense or combination of senses that enables him to "place" an object by internal evidence.

And in glass collecting that is frequently the only evidence any one has to go by, in the absence of a duly authenticated pedigree for a given piece. More and more as research is conducted into the history of the early glass houses and their products we realize how difficult it is to ascribe any type exclusively to a definite factory.

There was a time, not long ago, when any piece of glass bearing the characteristics of "Wistarberg" was classified as "Wistar" glass, but with a growing realization of how far the influence of the Wistars spread beyond their own factory, the collector who is a stickler for accuracy hesitates to give the name to any piece of glass unless it has an authentic history leading straight back to the factory at Wistarberg.

We know now that workers from the Wistar glass house left (much against the wishes of their employers) and went off to sell their services to others or to start up in business for themselves; and there is no reason to suppose that as soon as they stepped over the sill of the Wistar works they forgot the methods and designs by which they had been working, and the technique in which they had been trained. Rather it seems logical to suppose that the people who secured the services of these workers by offering increased pay made their offers with the definite end in view of getting exactly the sort of thing the men were able to deliver—that is, a knowledge of the methods used by the Wistars and the ability to produce glass of similar quality and design.

There are certain definite characteristics that mark the products known to have come from the Wistarberg factory, and if a piece of old glass possesses these characteristics it may truthfully be classed as in the Wistar tradition, whether it came from the Wistar works or from some other glass house where Wistar-trained men were employed. However, lacking an authentic history connecting it definitely with Wistarberg, the collector who is exceedingly careful in the matter of nomenclature now prefers to call it South Jersey or even, more safely, simply Early American.

Wistarberg is generally credited with being the first successful flint glass house established on American soil, and it is certain that it set fashions in glass that the people of the eighteenth century accepted with sufficient acclaim to make the venture a paying one for more than forty years.

The glass made by the Wistars for table or ornamental use was colored as well as clear and opaque white. More often than not, when colored glass was used, only one color was put into a single object; but not infrequently two or more colors were combined.

A characteristic of Wistar glass that strikes the eye almost at once is the shape. The first glass workers in Wistarberg, being from Rotterdam, naturally brought with them Dutch traditions. As a result Wistarberg bowls and pitchers are inclined to be broad of base and spreading of top, outlines that in any substance less ethereal looking than glass might give the effect of solidity or even stolidity. As it is, the light, shining through the clear curved expanse, or reflected back from the surface, takes away all feeling of weight; and a typical Wistar bowl in the beautiful green that was one of the favorite colors of the factory suggests a substance as light as a bubble or as mobile as water.

# Wistars and South Jersey Glass

A typical method of decoration used in the Wistarberg works was a thread of glass wound spirally around the object or applied to make the outlines of flowers, lily pads, etc. Another well-known Wistar decoration was the wave design, formed by applying a coating of soft glass to a partly finished object and drawing it, while still plastic, across the surface, so that it gave the effect of a breaking wave. A third scheme of decoration was the introduction of whorls of a contrasting color into the body of the object.

A wide range of color was used by the Wistar and other South Jersey glass houses—blue, principally in light shades, amber, brown in various tones, and especially green ranging from a faint tint to a deep emerald.

Structural marks considered characteristic of South Jersey glass are the crimped foot and the threaded neck.

One of the principal offshoots of the Wistar works was started in 1775 when some glass blowers named Stenger, young Germans who had broken away from their indenture to the Wistars, set up in business for themselves in Glassboro, New Jersey, on a piece of land from which they had cleared the pine timber. Although the new firm had a reasonable success for a few years, the depreciation of the Continental currency, which in 1780 fell to about three cents on a dollar in gold, forced them into bankruptcy. Whereupon, following the naïve custom of the day, because they could not pay their debts they were thrown into jail, where all possibility of regaining solvency would seem to be eliminated.

At all events, they drop out of the record at this point, and the best reason for mentioning them here is that they furnish an example of the way in which the Wistar influence was spread beyond the boundaries of Alloways-town. It is probable that the Stengers made only bottles during the five or six years of their venture, but there is no proof that they did not make tableware for themselves or toys and novelties to be sold or given to their neighbors.

This custom of making odd pieces as a "side line" was common in the early days, and we no doubt owe many of the most interesting and individual pieces now treasured to the initiative of some skilled glass blower who stayed after hours to fashion a bit for his own use or to serve as a gift.

At all events, these Stengers have the distinction of founding the earliest glass making establishment that has continued to make glass to the present day. The year after their failure the property was sold and under various names was conducted as an independent factory until 1918, when it was absorbed by the Owens Bottle Company of Toledo, Ohio.

When Caspar Wistar died in 1752 he left the Wistar-

WISTARBERG GREEN GLASS BOWL.    A TYPICAL WISTAR SHAPE

A VERY RARE WISTARBERG BOTTLE, APPARENTLY ONE OF THE OLDEST MADE
BY WISTAR. DUG OUT OF THE BOTTOM OF ALLOWAY CREEK, SALEM COUNTY,
N. J., IT SHOWS THE EFFECT OF LONG SUBMERGENCE IN THE IRIDESCENCE
RESULTING FROM THE ACTION OF MOISTURE AND CARBONIC GAS

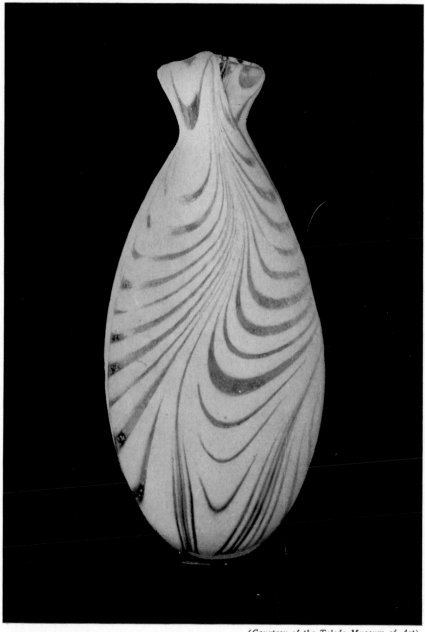

*(Courtesy of the Toledo Museum of Art)*

WISTARBERG DOUBLE FLASK, TURQUOISE AND OPAQUE WHITE GLASS
SHOWING THE CHARACTERISTIC WHORLS

(*Courtesy of the Metropolitan Museum of Art*)

WISTARBERG PITCHER

LATE EIGHTEENTH CENTURY WISTARBERG GLASS

berg works to his son, Richard, who, however, did not conduct them himself but put them under the charge of a manager. They were run successfully until about 1780. At that time, as already mentioned, the industry was feeling the effects of the war-time depression, Richard Wistar was getting old and had money enough so that he did not need the receipts from his glass making, and the fires of Wistarberg were allowed to die after a successful career of more than forty years.

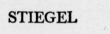

# STIEGEL

# Chapter Four

SECOND to the Wistars in time, but first, perhaps, in prestige, is the magnificent "Baron" Stiegel. When interest was first beginning to be revived in the works of this early and too long forgotten artist, it was customary to refer to him in straightforward manner as Baron Stiegel; but since the publication of the fascinating volume "Stiegel Glass," by Frederick William Hunter, it has become the fashion to enclose the title in quotation marks.

Whether this naïvely vain young German deliberately encouraged his associates to confer on him a title to which he was not born, or whether it was thrust upon him in the generous manner of the provincial American, who even to-day is inclined to dub every druggist "Doctor" and every village justice "Judge," the fact is that no one seems able to find any real evidence that Stiegel was entitled to be called "Baron."

However, no real patent of nobility could add luster to his scintillating personality, and no respect for Blind Justice, dealing out her rewards to extravagance, can take away from the pathos of his end—poor, almost friendless, eking out a precarious living by preaching, giving music lessons and teaching school.

[ 35 ]

It is probable that the impulse to make glass was in the blood of the young man who on August 31, 1750, landed in Philadelphia, one of two hundred and seventy emigrants brought by the ship *Nancy* from Rotterdam. He was twenty-one years old at this time, and his life heretofore had been spent in the place of his birth, near Cologne, where glass making had been carried on with more or less continuity since the days of the Romans. He signed his name on the ship's roster as Heinrich Wil. Stiegel, and made no claim to a title. The records fail to show that he brought with him any fortune other than an active brain and a sublime confidence in himself.

This confidence was apparently well founded, and he soon gave evidence of being what we should now refer to as a quick worker. Within two years he had married Elizabeth Huber, daughter of a prosperous owner of an iron furnace in Brickerville, Pennsylvania, and soon became a partner in his father-in-law's enterprises. In 1757 he built himself a new furnace which he called Elizabeth Furnace in honor of his wife.

With the versatility and energy that were to characterize his actions later in the glass industry, he branched out into various lines, apparently prospering in all his undertakings and giving every evidence of being on the way to a rich and resplendent old age.

How the decision to become a glass master came into

*(Courtesy of the Toledo Museum of Art)*

STIEGEL URN. BLUE GLASS WITH OPAQUE WHITE
RIM ON FOOT, TOP, AND FINIAL ON COVER

STIEGEL GLASS. 1, ENAMELED TUMBLERS; 2, TINTED SUGAR BOWL; 3, ENAMELED MUG; 4, ENGLISH GLASS VASE, RESEMBLING STIEGEL; 5, ENAMELED BOTTLE.

(Courtesy of the Toledo Museum of Art)

his mind the records fail to tell, but in 1763 he began to experiment in the making of glass at Elizabeth Furnace; and Mr. Hunter thinks it is probable that the relatively crude pieces produced at that time were the cause of a statement made by Governor John Penn, of Pennsylvania, that "There is a glass house in Lancaster County, but it makes only a little coarse ware for the county neighbors."

In the account books of Charming Forge, one of Stiegel's plants, which Mr. Hunter had an opportunity to examine, he found a record of sums drawn in 1763 and 1764 to cover the expense of a trip to Bristol, England, then one of the centers of glass making. When he returned, Stiegel brought with him both English and German glass workers and began glass making in earnest.

He laid out a whole town which he called Mannheim and populated with the workers in his glass houses, whom he treated with a consideration rather in advance of the custom of the day, and who in return accorded him a sort of feudal loyalty. The factory prospered so that Stiegel, in a letter to a friend, wrote that it brought him an income of £5,000, a sum at that time worth many times its present value.

With this great increase in prosperity Stiegel's natural bent toward magnificence developed rapidly. He seems to have been one of those men, who are to be found in every generation, gifted, enthusiastic, and self-confident, to whom success comes too early and too easily. Not content to live on the really princely income that was his, he began to accumulate real estate in great parcels, borrowing recklessly and without reckoning the final repayment, and conducting his domestic affairs on a basis suited to the baron, or even the prince, of a fairy story.

He built himself a mansion at Mannheim and two tall towers, one at Elizabeth Furnace and another at Schaefferstown. A cannon was placed on each tower and a third on the band platform of his Mannheim house, from which he entertained the villagers with concerts, provided by imported musicians and by talented inhabitants of the village whom he selected and trained.

When he traveled from one of his houses to another, he drove in a gorgeous coach with eight white horses, and outriders, and couriers to go before. His arrival and departure were announced by the firing of the cannon, and the wondering and admiring people of the countryside were probably only too willing to accord him any title of nobility that pleased him.

During this period of his magnificence he interested himself in the spiritual welfare of his neighbors, sometimes preaching to them from the chapel in his mansion; and he gave a lot to a board of trustees and on it erected Zion Lutheran Church, which he donated in consideration

of a nominal rental, the most noteworthy item being one
red rose yearly. His downfall occurred not long after
this gift, and the payment of the rose was allowed to
lapse until a few years ago, when it was revived with
enthusiasm; and every year on the second Sunday in
June Mannheim celebrates the anniversary with a pomp
and ceremony that would have delighted Stiegel's heart.

It has been frequently pointed out by the thrifty that,
however magnificent an income may be, if it is exceeded
by the expenditures the result is penury; and that was
the way with Stiegel. In 1774, the crash which had been
impending for some time, came with devastating force;
Stiegel was declared a bankrupt, his glass works was sold
by the sheriff, and he himself was imprisoned.

This was a crushing bit of reality to Stiegel, and, although he was released by special act of the legislature,
the vital spark that had made his early success was lost.
The rest of his life is a cloud-covered journey, in which
we catch glimpses of a stricken man, acting as foreman
in one of the iron works he had formerly owned, earning
small sums by teaching the elements of music to the
children of his former employees, working, striving, and
never losing hope that somehow, from some miraculous
source, the means would be provided for him to rise
again to the crest of the wave. The miracle failed to
materialize and when death came, at the comparatively

youthful age of fifty-six, Stiegel was buried in an unmarked grave, the location of which is not known with certainty. So, he takes his place among that band of artists and creators who have found disappointment and frustration in life but have won a recrudescence through their works after many years.

The products of Stiegel's works included the staples of the day, window glass and bottles, but the articles that collectors are most interested in are the tableware and ornaments he produced. We know from advertisements that he made a great variety of shapes. One of these advertisements appeared in the *Pennsylvania Gazette*, June 27, 1771, inserted by a merchant of Philadelphia, as follows:

### STIEGEL GLASS

This is to acquaint the public and my kind customers in particular, that I have lately been at the Glass Factory in Mannheim, in Lancaster County, and contracted with Mr. William Henry Stiegel for a large and complete assortment of his Flint Glass, consisting of quart, pint, half-pint, gill, and half-gill tumblers, wine glasses; vinegar glasses, salt cellars, cream pots, sugar dishes with covers; jelly glasses, syllabub glasses; proof bottles, etc., etc., to be delivered to me immediately at my house in Market Street, next door to the Indian King, where I

ENAMELED STIEGEL GLASS.  DOVE DESIGN ON THE FLIP

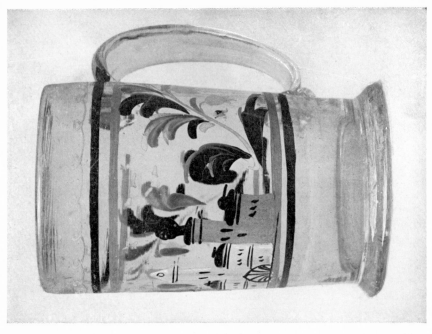

STIEGEL GLASS OF THE EIGHTEENTH CENTURY

STIEGEL CLEAR GLASS SUGAR BOWL

(*Courtesy of the Metropolitan Museum of Art*)

will sell them as low, or lower and equal in quality with my flint glass imported from England. Any orders shall be punctually complied with, and as quickly forwarded, and will be exactly furnished.

Wanted—A Glass Cutter and Grinder, such a workman by applying will meet with good encouragement.
ALEXANDER BARTRAM.

Another advertisement, issued by Caullman and Fegan, who had a store in Second Street, Philadelphia, "fifth door from Race Street," went still further into details, and enumerated:

"Double and single flint gallon, three quart, half gallon, and single quart decanters with stoppers; sugar loaf ditto; round ditto; single and double flint tumblers pint measure, half pint ditto and gills; tall pint tumblers, pints and half pints; enamelled mason wines; enamelled twisted mason wines; plain ditto, common wines; twisted ditto, enamelled ditto; syllabubs, with one handle, ditto with two handles; bubbled buttoned jellies; common acorn ditto; jacony salts, and enamelled ditto; double and single cruets with stoppers; tall, twisted and enamelled cruets; enamelled three footed creams, common ditto; three footed salts, enamelled blue and plain; inks of all sorts; and flower pots; garden pots; proof glasses; lemonade jars; candlesticks, ornamented; servers, ornamented; common and enamelled mustards; vinegar and oil cruets, joined together; and great variety of glasses, too tedious to insert.

"The public may rest assured that no other kind of glass will be kept, or sold in said store. From the great experience that the proprietor of this manufactory, Mr. William Henry Stiegel, has of the patriotic spirit of the Gentlemen in Pennsylvania, and the provinces adjacent, he flatters himself that it will meet with suitable encouragement. All orders of patrons sent to the store, shall be accurately forwarded and complied with, at the Manufactory, or at the Store, from time to time. All Store-keepers, Tavern-keepers, and Retailers, will be completely supplied to orders, lower than importation price."

These articles and the others "too tedious to insert," were produced in clear flint, and some of them were made in green of varying shades, in wine colored glass, in amethyst, and in blue, the favorite color of Stiegel and the color most frequently used in his glass works. There were also numerous articles in clear and colored flint flashed with opaque white, and some bi-colored, such as clear flint with blue, opaque white with blue, and clear flint with amethyst.

Stiegel had in his employ skilled decorators in various lines. They embellished his wares with engraving and enameled designs which soon placed the output of the

Mannheim works on a par with the best that was being made in Europe.

According to Mr. Hunter "a few of the distinguishing characteristics of Stiegel Glass, over and above the high structural tension and resultant resonance and brittleness characteristic of all early flint glass, are a nice taste and discrimination in the use of essentially beautiful and artistic patterns, a sound sense of form and a consistent adherence to pure lines in the designing of its shapes, a general lightness of weight and a habitual thinness of texture, a beautiful brilliance of surface and a remarkable uniformity of color; and finally, a quality difficult to define, yet once found never to be mistaken or misprized, a quality especially noticeable in those endlessly varying individual specimens of a few characteristic shapes and decorations, where the condensed pattern was impressed upon the glass in a small pattern-mold and the article then blown by hand in the open air, a quality that it is perhaps only possible here to call the Spirit of the Handmade in its distinguishing Stiegel incarnation."

It is this delicacy and beauty of manipulation that distinguishes Stiegel glass, that gives it the indefinable something which we feel at once and which grows upon us as we become more and more familiar with the work of this artist-glassmaker. The Stiegel blue, at its best, is the bluest, and the Stiegel amethyst the richest deep violet that one can ever hope to see. Little wonder then when a piece of genuine Stiegel comes into the market it brings a fabulous price and is cherished by the fortunate owner as a rare and valued treasure.

# SANDWICH GLASS

FOUR PIECES OF OPAL SANDWICH GLASS

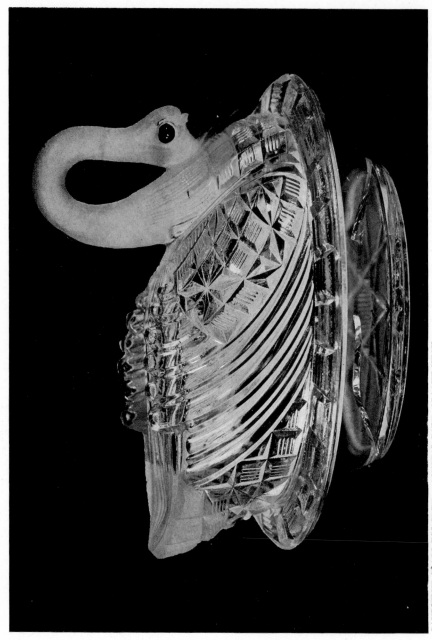

SANDWICH GLASS EGG DISH. CRYSTAL BODY, OPAQUE NECK, AND REDDISH COLORED BILL AND EYES

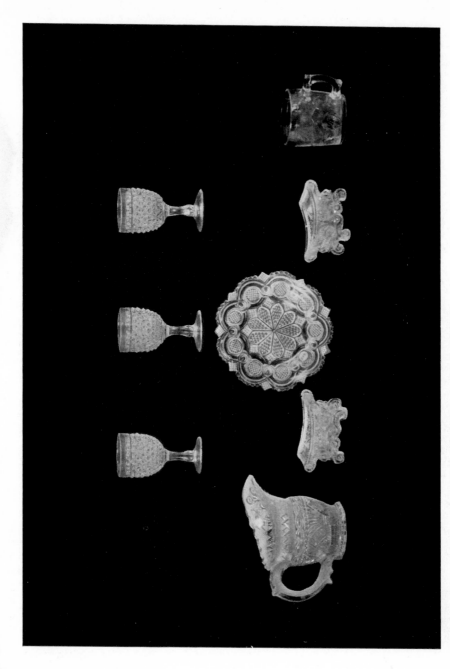

HOB-NAIL WINE GLASSES—SANDWICH CREAMERS—EARLY SANDWICH
SALTS—BULL'S EYE "TODDY PLATE"—CHERRY PATTERN MUG

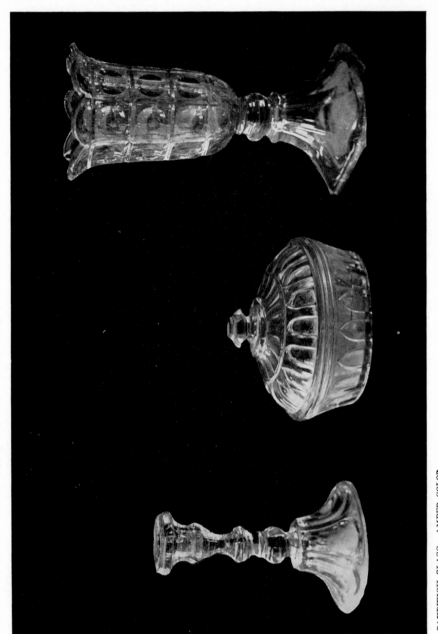

## Chapter Five

AFTER mention of Wistar and Stiegel, the natural step is to go on to Sandwich glass. At mention of Sandwich, one usually thinks of pressed glass, but as a matter of fact blown glass was made at the Boston and Sandwich Glass Works during most if not all of its existence, and for the first few years of its life blown glass was the only kind made.

In his "Reminiscences of Glass Making," Deming Jarves tells briefly of the beginning of this famous glass house.

"In 1825," he writes, "a Flint-Glass Manufactory was established by individual enterprise in Sandwich, Mass. Ground was broke in April, dwellings for the workmen built, and manufactory completed; and on the 4th day of July, 1825, they commenced blowing glass—three months from first breaking ground. In the following year it was purchased of the proprietor, a company formed, and incorporated under the title of Boston and Sandwich Glass Company."

According to Mr. Charles Messer Stow, who has done some interesting research in connection with the Sand-

wich works, the "individual enterprise" to which the
founding of the company was due was Mr. Jarves' own
enterprise. He was in many ways a progressive and for-
ward-looking man, a resident of Boston, who had learned
the glass business through connection with the New England Glass Company. Mr. Stow's account of the beginning of the undertaking is that Mr. Jarves, who was
very fond of the country about Sandwich, on Cape Cod,
called a meeting of its citizens and told them of a trip
he had recently made through Pennsylvania and Ohio.
One interesting fact he had noted was that the glass
workers in Pittsburgh were making from two to two and
a half dollars a day, and he said that if the people of
Sandwich were sufficiently interested to warrant the
undertaking he would build glass works and furnish
employment for many of the men of the village.

Two dollars a day was "big money" at that time; the
response was sufficiently enthusiastic, and the building
was put through in record time, as related by Mr. Jarves.
The rest of the history up to 1850 is given succinctly by
Mr. Jarves.

"Like their predecessors, they commenced in a small
way; beginning with an eight-pot furnace, each holding
eight hundred pounds. The weekly melts at that period
did not exceed seven thousand pounds, and yearly product
seventy-five thousand dollars; giving employment to from

sixty to seventy hands. From time to time, as their business warranted, they increased their capital until it reached the present sum of four hundred thousand dollars. Their weekly melts have increased from seven thousand pounds to much over one hundred thousand pounds; their hands employed from seventy to over five hundred; their one furnace of eight pots to four furnaces of ten pots; and yearly product from seventy-five thousand dollars to six hundred thousand dollars."

The metal used in the Sandwich works was of good quality, and the glass had a great brilliancy, due, it is said, to the presence of barytes in the batch. The products of Sandwich soon came to be noted for this quality and for the clear ringing tone when struck. If it had continued to be only a producer of blown glass, however, we should in all probability have to record it merely as one of the many glass houses running at the time. It owes its distinction to the fact that it was the first glass house to adopt and perfect the method of manipulating glass by pressure instead of by blowing.

It is customary to credit this factory with the invention of the pressing process, but, as noted in the introduction, pressing is almost as ancient as blowing, and articles of pressed glass are found in the old Egyptian tombs. Moreover, Deming Jarves himself disclaims the credit for its invention. Under the heading "Pressed Glass," he wrote:

"This important branch of glass-making demands more than a passing notice. Although it is commonly believed here that the invention originated in this country, the claim cannot be fully sustained. Fifty years back," (this was written in 1850) "the writer imported from Holland salts made by being pressed in metallic moulds, and from England glass candlesticks and table centre-bowls, plain, with pressed square feet, rudely made, somewhat after the present mode of moulding. From 1814 to 1838, no improvement was made in Europe in this process, which was confined to common salts and square feet. . . . America can claim the credit of great improvements in the needful machinery which has advanced the art to its present perfection."

The first experiment was made with a rude press, invented by Deming Jarves and the workman who had suggested the experiment to him. This was constructed of wood and had one serious disadvantage, for when the hot fluid was dropped into it it scorched and spoiled the article. Later, a steel mold was designed to prevent this mishap.

The new product caught the popular fancy and quickly became the chief output of the Sandwich plant. Enormous quantities of glass were pressed in these works, so numerous that it would be impossible to list them all even if we had a complete record of the patterns made at Sandwich, as, alas, we have not. They varied in color, and beautiful designs in vases, cup plates, door knobs, cologne bottles, lamps, candlesticks, etc., were much in demand. Many of the patterns were designed by Hiram Dillaway, an Englishman, who was for a long time the head mold maker.

The first tumbler made by this process was kept as a curiosity, but unfortunately was broken at the Centennial Celebration where it was sent for exhibition.

That the Sandwich Company made glass in every conceivable design was proven by the collection formerly owned by a lady whose father had an interest in the works. He fitted out his daughter on her wedding day with a specimen of every piece made in the factory, so that her closets were full to overflowing. Indeed, she had so much of it that she attached little or no value to the pieces, and one by one they were given away or exchanged for glittering new cut glass. To-day only a few pieces remain, but these give an indication of the value of the collection. Among the remaining pieces is a rare pink sugar bowl with matching pitcher. Alas! The rest of the set was broken or given away long years before its value as an antique was appreciated.

One of the interesting pieces made by the factory was a marvelous bowl, designed as a gift for Daniel Webster. Six months were required for the making, as a mold had to be prepared especially for the purpose. Where the bowl has gone no one can discover, but the memory of it lingers still in the hearts of all glass enthusiasts, and the faint hope of finding it some day, in some forgotten corner of the world, is the lodestar of many collectors.

The Sandwich Company developed a great export trade. In later years they sent their lamps all over the world, so that the inhabitants of the remote islands and corners of the globe may be pictured as reading their various languages under the beneficent rays of a lamp from Cape Cod. Cruets were another specialty and tumblers they turned out in enormous quantities.

The end of this company was one of those unlooked for events that sometimes happen when continuity seems so assured that nothing else enters any one's mind. In the early eighties the company was employing about three hundred men and boys, most of the men owning their own homes, and all the workers well paid and prosperous. A sudden acute situation which rose in the relations between employers and workers came to a head in 1887. The directors of the company, which had been running at a loss for some time, issued an ultimatum to the workers. If the fires were allowed to die, they declared, no new fires would be kindled. The men were unable to believe that this was a possibility, and the fires went out. The directors were as good as their word and the glass works at Sandwich have been a thing of the past for nearly forty years.

The specimens of Sandwich in which collectors are most interested are those that were turned out during the first twenty-five or thirty years of the company's existence. This was the period when Deming Jarves was an active force in the works and his influence was felt in the quality of the metal as well as in the charm of the design. In 1858, after a quarrel with the directors, he withdrew, and formed the Cape Cod Glass Works, to run in opposition with his old company. This firm was never very influential, however, and did not last long after the death of Deming Jarves in 1869.

It was during this early period that the Sandwich works made the great assortment of cup plates which are now so much in demand. This was also the period of experimentation in the pressing of glass, and some of the early pieces show the results of inexperience. Specimens of one of the rarest types of cup plates, a Bunker Hill design, are imperfect owing to the fact that there was not enough glass dropped into the mold, and as a result the plunger did not force it into contact with the outer mold at all points.

It was in these early years, too, that the most desirable of the lamps and candlesticks were made; those

[ 53 ]

petal top candlesticks with a loop base and a scarred bottom in almost every possible color—white, clear and opaque, pale lavender, purple, blue, green, yellow and opalescent. Some of them were made of blue and white combined. The most rare of all perhaps are the dark amber.

This was the time when the dolphin group of candlesticks was developed in greatest perfection. This design was no doubt copied from some of the imported pieces brought over by Deming Jarves to serve as patterns and suggestions to his designers. Happy the collector who can boast a pair of Sandwich candlesticks in dolphin design!

About 1850 the whale oil lamps began to be made. The earliest type was of simple design in clear glass. Later more elaborate ones were produced. Sometimes ornate lamp bowls were imported and joined to Sandwich glass bases.

A characteristic method of treatment was the finish known sometimes as snakeskin and sometimes as lace glass. This is a stippled background used with much delicacy in the early Sandwich pieces. A later use of the device was more clumsily handled, so that the beauty and delicacy of the early background were lacking.

The later pressed glass from Sandwich was in most respects inferior to the early product, due largely to the substitution of machine made molds for the early hand cut ones, and to a greater elaboration of design which descended sometimes to an effect very close to tawdryness.

Color was one of the Sandwich specialties and some of the colors were produced in a perfection that no other glass house of the time could attain. Recently an old notebook of Deming Jarves has come to light which gives some of the color secrets used in the making of Sandwich glass, but these are of more interest to practical glass mixers than to collectors, so I will not take space to give the details here.

Unfortunately the company seems to have found such a ready market that they did not resort to advertising, so we have no such comprehensive lists of the products as we have through the advertisements of Wistar and Stiegel glass. There is a tradition that there was a pattern book, kept at the factory, in which was filed the design of every piece ever turned out; and this, if it is still in existence, may some day come to light. One can well imagine the excitement that will be created if it does!

# OTHER EARLY GLASS HOUSES

## Chapter Six

A FACT that stands out more and more clearly, as research is carried on in the field of American glass, is that glass making in the second half of the eighteenth and the first half of the nineteenth centuries was almost as widespread, in proportion to the population and development of the country, as it is to-day; and that when one has mentioned Wistar, Stiegel and Sandwich glass, he has by no means covered the ground, even if the enumeration is to be confined to glass makers of the first rank.

In the book "Old Glass, European and American," by N. Hudson Moore, the author lists over a hundred glass factories in operation in this country before 1850. Some of them lasted only a short time; others, though long since dead, ran for many years. It must be remembered that, however short the duration of a glass factory, while it was in operation it was turning out glass in considerable quantities. This was distributed not only into the homes of those who lived near the centers of production and distribution, but went in peddler's carts to the remote hilltops and valleys where the housewives of farms and villages spent their treasured savings for still more treasured bits of glassware to ornament the corner cupboard or the "sitting-room whatnot," or to grace the dinner or "tea" table on special occasions.

Some of these now almost forgotten factories were acknowledged leaders among their contemporaries. Deming Jarves, a most generous competitor, does not claim first place for the Sandwich works in either pressed or blown glass.

Antedating the Sandwich factory was the New England Glass Company of Boston, in which Deming Jarves learned the business. This factory made blown glass, and later pressed glass, very similar in character to the product of the Sandwich company. Speaking of the New England Company Jarves says:

"That company, from 1817 to the present time, (1850) have pursued the business with signal success; beginning with the small capital of forty thousand dollars, they have from time to time increased it, until it amounts at the present time to half a million of dollars. . . . They now run five furnaces, averaging ten pots to each, capacity of two thousand pounds to each pot. They employ over five hundred men and boys, and the yearly product is not less than five hundred thousand dollars."

It is easy to see that during all these years this company must have sent out a vast quantity of glass, much of which it would be impossible to tell from the product of Sandwich. It is said that the Sandwich glass was more brilliant than that of the New England Glass Works owing to the presence of barytes in the Sandwich glass; but there is no proof that this was never used by the other company, and in all other respects the output of the two factories was so similar that even experts hesitate to ascribe certain pieces to one or the other, lacking a definite history of the piece.

Speaking of another competitor, John L. Gillerland, Jarves writes:

"In 1823 Gillerland dissolved the connection" (with the firm of Fisher and Gillerland) "and built, on his own account, a manufactory in Brooklyn, N. Y., which he conducts at this period with great skill and success, and is considered the best metal mixer in the United States."

Speaking of him again further on in the book, Jarves said:

"John L. Gillerland, late of the Brooklyn Glass Works, is remarkably skillful in mixing metal. He has succeeded in producing the most brilliant glass of refractory power, which is so difficult to obtain. A gold medal was awarded his glass, in face of European competition, at the Great International Exhibition in London, 1852."

Evidently Jarves was mixed in his dates, for the great exhibition was held in London in 1851, but this does not change the fact that at that exposition Gillerland did indeed carry off the gold medal.

Speaking of pressed glass, Jarves wrote:

"It is, however, conceded that James B. Lyon and Co. of Pittsburgh, stand first. To such a degree of delicacy and fineness have they carried their manufacture, that only experts in the trade can distinguish between their straw-stem wines, and other light and beautiful articles made in moulds, and those blown by the most skilled workmen. . . . Lyon and Co. also excel all other American firms in large ware for table services, as well as in the more delicate objects of use."

Later, in 1867, this same James B. Lyon, took first prize for his exhibit of pressed glass at the Paris Exposition.

Moreover, these skilled glass workers to whom Jarves paid his tribute do not by any means cover the field. There were any number of other firms that made both pressed and blown glass of great excellence. There is not space here to mention even the names of all that deserve mention, but a few details about some of them will help to emphasize the fact already mentioned that American glass comes from many places, and that the ascribing of a piece to a definite factory is a difficult and often impossible task. It also emphasizes the fact that the lack of a pedigree need not lessen the value of a piece. If it has

A PAIR OF LARGE PITCHERS, BLOWN BY MATT JOHNSON AT STODDARD, N. H.

GLASS JARS MADE AT STODDARD, N. H.

the qualities that mark good work it is worth having whether it came from Sandwich, Mannheim, or Wistarberg or from Pittsburgh, Albany or Saratoga.

There were two glass houses at Keene, New Hampshire, during the first half of the nineteenth century, one running from 1814 to 1850, and the other from 1815 to 1842. Connected with both of these works were members of the Schoolcraft family, a name prominent in the glass industry in this country. Later in the century, glass works were established at Stoddard, New Hampshire. The glass made at both Keene and Stoddard was dark and coarse in texture but specimens are scarce and highly valued. Some interesting three mold pieces were made at Stoddard. They were not of the light clear flint which is commonly thought of in connection with three mold pieces, but they have a certain attraction of their own. Specimens of Stoddard glass are to be seen at the Toledo Museum of Art and at the Metropolitan Museum of Art.

New York State early figured in glass making. As in the case of every other section of the country, many of the early attempts were of short duration and little importance, except as steps in the ladder that leads from the small beginnings to the present condition of the industry with its multiple and highly specialized activities. The elder Schoolcraft, who has been mentioned in connection with the Keene works, was superintendent of a factory near Albany, New York, before he went to Keene, about 1814.

In 1835 the New York Census reported thirteen glass factories in the state. One of these, situated at Saratoga, was making bottles, some of them for the spring water for which the town is famous, others pocket flasks. These flasks are highly valued at present as are numerous small novelties and dishes made by the workmen "on their own" for their own use or as gifts. The metal was all green, but of good quality and was made in three shades, light green, olive, and a deep rich green, almost the color of an emerald. The shapes of the articles made by these workers were graceful and the workmanship excellent, so that any piece of this ware that is obtainable is well worth adding to a collection.

A factory that made articles much in demand at present was started in Millville, New Jersey, about 1820. Other prominent works were located at Salisbury, Vermont; at West Willington, Connecticut; at Wheeling, Virginia; at Louisville, Kentucky; and, besides the factories already mentioned in Pennsylvania, there were numerous works of great importance which space does not allow me to describe in detail.

During the second half of the nineteenth century the vogue for cut glass became acute and great industries were built up on this one phase of the industry. In this same period many changes were introduced in the methods of manufacture of all sorts of glass, which made it possible to employ it for many more uses than ever before in the history of the world. At the same time modern laboratory methods of testing, together with modern machinery, made it possible to produce it in quantity and variety never before attained. The subject of glass in industrial use is a fascinating one, but not within the scope of this book, except in the briefest mention. A scanning of the different kinds of glass in which modern factories specialize names such varieties as these to spur our imagination:

*Unshatterable and laminated; rough and ribbed; bullet proof, glass for scientific instruments, surfaced to give pure spectral colors; acid stippled glass; actinic glass, excluding harmful sun rays; heat intercepting; fluted window glass; tail light lenses; signal semaphores; light diffuser glass; and goggle glass, all colors.*

One outstanding achievement in the field of American glass manufacture has been the perfecting of plate glass, which, according to Deming Jarves, had never been successfully made in this country before 1850.

But, in spite of the benefits conferred on us by the perfecting of mechanical equipment, which makes glass available for so many uses undreamed of by our forebears, those of us who love beauty, who cherish the marks of individuality that lift an article out of the realm of the artizan into the world of the artist, are grateful for the craftsmen who in this up to date age are keeping alive the fire that burned for the glass makers of ancient Egypt. This fire, that burned steadily through the ages, sometimes obscured for a time, again blazing sublimely as in Venice and other places, is still kept burning in this country and is producing articles of beauty that a hundred or perhaps a thousand years from now may be bringing to the Americans of that day the same delight that the lovely vases of Stiegel and Wistar are bringing to us of this twentieth century.

# AMERICAN BOTTLES

## Chapter Seven

BOTTLE blowing in America has a long and honorable history, ranging from the time when, in 1608, they were first blown in the heart of the Jamestown forest, until to-day when they comprise every imaginable variety and color. A collection of the various periods shows the evolution and depicts graphically the growth of glass manufacture in America. Fortunately, before the old bottles were entirely demolished, interest was awakened, and to-day both collectors and historians are searching far and wide for unusual specimens, realizing that a complete representation would illustrate an important phase in the glass history of our country.

It is sometimes difficult to determine the period of bottles which now and then come to light, unearthed from old cellars or attics. Colors and sizes vary so much that they are not a good test, but we know that the earliest American bottles were rough and irregular at the edge of the mouth, where, while the glass was in a plastic state, it was cut with shears, leaving no rim or ornament. Another indication of age is found on the base where the pontil mark was usually left all rough, just as it looked

[ 69 ]

when the bottle was broken from the pontil bar which held it while the workman was shaping the neck.

The earliest types were slender and arched in formation with edges horizontally corrugated. Bottles blown at a slightly later period, were generally oval-shaped with edges ribbed vertically. Following this fashion came the circular type with plain rounded edges. Other pieces blown of this period show a suggestion of collar at the mouth.

Bottles with smooth and hollow bases were blown during the period immediately preceding the Civil War, a development made possible by a new process which employed a "snap" or case instead of the pontil for holding the bottle. Following other changes in methods, the mouths of the bottles were finished with rims, which added much to their appearance. The decorative schemes were worked out in transparent white, pale blue, sapphire blue, light green, emerald green, olive, brown or claret.

A little later in the century came the calabash or decanter shapes, no longer flattened or shallow, but almost spherical with edges that showed vertical corrugation, ribbing or fluting. These had long slender necks with finishing caps at the mouth and were scarred at the base.

After this the bottles were arched in formation, deep and flattened, displaying vertically corrugated edges, and short broad necks capped with round and narrow heads,

with the bases either scarred or flattened. This type of
bottle was generally in use until the modern flask dis-
placed it.

An interesting type of bottles, from the collector's
point of view, are the great "carboys" used for many
years to hold vinegar, cider, or "Apple Jack." Most of
these that remain to us to-day are green in color, of varying sizes and shapes. In his enlightening volume "Glass
Making in All Ages" Walter Rosenhain tells us:

"Large objects like carboys were difficult to blow on
account of the weight of glass to be handled by the
gatherer and blower. In the old days the only aid available to the blower was the method of injecting into the
partially blown carboy a small quantity of either water
or alcohol. As this liquid vaporized immediately when
exposed to the heat of the glass, if the blower held his
thumb over the opening in the blow-pipe, the force of the
vapor was able to blow out the molten glass to the proper
extent."

In no other direction can the bottle collector find such
variety as in the pursuit of the decorated bottles which
flooded the country during the middle third of the nineteenth century. Enterprising European potters were
making a form of picture-ware known as Liverpool. This
included pictorial representations of many of the political and historical events in our country. These plates

and tea sets were so novel and attractive that they immediately became the fashion. Manufacturers in this country were quick to copy the idea in glass and soon vied
with one another in producing new designs in bottles to
please the popular fancy.

Competition was keen and resulted in the multiplicity
of interesting designs which we are hunting for at the
present day. So many and varied were the subjects used
that America seemed for a while to have gone bottle mad.
The decorations ranged from simple floral wreaths to
elaborate, complicated borders introduced in high relief
around opportune sketches and quotations, representations of contemporary events, all of which made strong
sentimental or patriotic appeal to the would-be pur-
chasers. These were blown in metal molds which had
previously been prepared by professional mold-cutters.

A study of these old bottles with a knowledge of the
reasons why they were so ornamented naturally arouses
interest in the heart of every collector and antiquarian
who is eager to add them to his collection. The first ones
designed were produced by the Kensington Glass Works
in Philadelphia, between 1833 and 1837, most of them
being dark amber in coloring.

The most noted bottle designs date from about the
middle of the last century and include such examples as

the Kossuth and Jenny Lind bottles, both of which are particularly well known, and much sought after.

In these days, when the name of Jenny Lind is only a name to most people, this old bottle is a concrete bit of evidence that helps the student of history to regain some sense of the fine frenzy of the time when a really great singer was so much a rarity in New York that the first seat for her first concert brought $225, a figure that was exceeded in other cities. From an old gentleman who was in charge of the Temple, where she sang during her stay in Boston, it was learned that it was her custom to come to the Temple every morning, so that she might familiarize herself with the acoustic properties of the interior. So idolized was she by the general public that the corridor through which it was hoped she would pass on her way out was crowded with an eager throng. She was advised of the fact and urged to leave by a side entrance, but when she found that they were people who could not afford the admission fee to her concerts she insisted upon using the public entrance and even stopped to shake hands with those who pressed around her, and to respond in gracious words to their greetings. To-day this would be called a publicity stunt, and perhaps it was, but it was one of the things which endeared this remarkable woman to the public and made it possible to sell thousands of

[ 73 ]

bottles bearing her portrait—bottles that to-day we are paying large prices to add to our collections.

One famous old bottle displays a horse drawing on rails a four wheeled cart loaded with bales of cotton and lumps of coal. It signalized the completion of the "Baltimore and Ohio Railroad" in 1830, a line which to-day seems hardly worth considering, as its total length was but fourteen miles. The design was impressed on a panel lengthwise of the bottle and the legend, "Success to the Railroad" was shown on the margin of the panel.

Between the years 1840 and 1860 every factory in the land produced the decorated bottle, many with all sorts of freak designs, novelties, jokes and advertising sketches on the surface. Old concerns like the Kensington Works, at Philadelphia, and the Whitney Glass Works, of Glassboro, New Jersey (now a part of the Owens Bottle Company of Toledo, Ohio), have in their collection eloquent samples of the passing fads of a quarter of a century. Then suddenly the bottle bubble burst and this storied type passed into oblivion, to be sought after and made valuable by collectors to-day.

All of the decorated bottles are interesting and some are illuminating. For instance there was a distiller named E. C. Booz in Philadelphia at the time of the "Log Cabin Campaign" of William Henry Harrison. The Whitney Company made bottles for this distiller in the shape of eight-inch-high log cabins, symbolizing the birthplace of Harrison, whose campaign for the presidency was one of the most heated in our history. The distiller's name was pressed into the bottle, and so effective was this simple advertising that the phrase "I'll take a bottle of Booz" came to mean just what the advertiser intended it should—a bottle of whiskey. These log cabin bottles are now exceedingly rare, and bring large prices when offered for sale.

Many of the early bottles depict not only important events but personages, including Presidents, and often a group of them representing varied scenes from the career of a single person presents what might well be termed his life history.

A bottle belonging to the "stormy thirties" carries a representation of Andrew Jackson arrayed in uniform with a choker which entirely hides his ears.

On another bottle is the portrait of Zachary Taylor with the words, "Taylor never surrenders" and on the Taylor-Bragg variety, the hardy old leader is represented saying, as he did at Buena Vista, "A little more grape, Captain Bragg."

There came into vogue also a great variety of miscellaneous decorative designs, flowers, fruit, cornucopias, rural scenes, fraternal emblems, particularly Masonic, dating from about 1848; ships and eight pointed stars, panels of fruit and grain. One had a bold Pike's Peak pilgrim with staff and bundle—signifying, of course, the first successful passage of the Rocky Mountains. Other interesting types are indicated in the specimen made by a Pittsburgh concern, which shows on one side an eagle, with monument and flag, and on the reverse in the foreground an Indian with bow and arrow shooting a bird, with a tree and a dog in the background. There was an almost infinite number of designs of these old glass products and the sincere collector wonders how many rare specimens are hidden away in old houses unknown to their occupants.

Ever and anon a hitherto undiscovered design appears from some obscure corner, showing extra-fancy ornamentation of animals, fishes, eggs, pickles, canteens, cigars, shells, pistols, violins, horns, lanterns, lassoes, prospectors' implements, and other equally commonplace articles of every day life.

Interesting specimens of American glass bottles are to be found all over the country in museums and private collections. Lifting them to the light one delights in the color which deepens at the thicker parts of the bottle, and with this pleasure in visioning its shimmering radiance comes the more subtle joy of handling one of the early forms of American art.

Some such treasures are to be found to-day in an old

tavern in Peterborough, New Hampshire, owned by Stephen Van Rensselaer, who has an invaluable collection of old glass, and who is a connoisseur on the subject. W. S. Walbridge of The Owens Bottle Company has also an enviable assortment of varied types, some of which are in a class not ordinarily sought by collectors. For example, there are several specimens of glass preserving jars in use previous to 1860. These range in size from small rough-mouthed cup-like pieces to tall jars resembling the modern milk bottle in shape. Other interesting pieces in his collection are old ink bottles with quills inserted, medicine bottles used by the big patent medicine and proprietary preparation concerns, a Toby bottle and one of Baltimore Monument type. One bottle is shaped like a domino block, another like a bear. A bottle in the form of a standing Indian was used as an advertisement for Indian bitters. One of the quaintest and most interesting shows Moses smiting the rock. Such freak bottles are valued as illustrations of a definite phase of American glass making.

Crude and clumsy these blue-green and amber-brown bottles may be, but they are precious as well, and every collector nurses a secret hope of eventually owning some such treasure as a "Glass Fish," a "Moses" or a "Santa Claus." One of Mr. Walbridge's chief treasures is a perfect Booz bottle presented to him by Mr. Dudley Whitney, a descendant of the Whitneys who originated the Whitney Glass Works and who was president of this Company at the time of his gift to Mr. Walbridge. This valuable bottle is light green in color and considered by experts to be a most unusual specimen. It was found at Glassboro, New Jersey, and still bears the label "E. M. Leeds, Drugs and Prescriptions, Glassboro."

Most unusual is a very rare Wistarberg bottle, which was taken from the bottom of Alloway Creek, Salem County, New Jersey, where the Wistarberg factory was located. This is apparently one of the oldest made at Wistarberg. It was given to Mr. Walbridge by J. Thomas Gaynor of Salem, New Jersey. The bottle is iridescent in coloring and shows traces of having been in the water for a very long time.

Probably the most exquisite of all the specimens which grace collections of American glass are those that were made by the artist glass maker Stiegel, who employed color in the engraving, and who for a time, manufactured Bohemian glass in his plant in Mannheim, Pennsylvania, ruby red, white and blue. It did seem a pity that in spite of the many beautiful things which came from his shop, "Baron" Stiegel failed in business within ten years. Like many another artist, however, a recognition of his genius came too late for him to profit by it.

Late in the eighteenth century fancy pocket flasks and

THE FAMOUS "BOOZ" BOTTLE,
A VERY UNUSUAL SPECIMEN OF THE OLD WHISKY BOTTLE.
IT IS LIGHT GREEN IN COLOR

MR. WALBRIDGE'S TREASURE OF MORE THAN THREE HUNDRED ANTIQUE AMERICAN
BOTTLES IS ONE OF THE MOST COMPLETE COLLECTIONS IN THE COUNTRY

SUCCESS TO THE RAILROAD, SHOWING A HORSE
DRAWING A FOUR-WHEELED CAR

THE EAGLE, A FAVORITE DECORATION

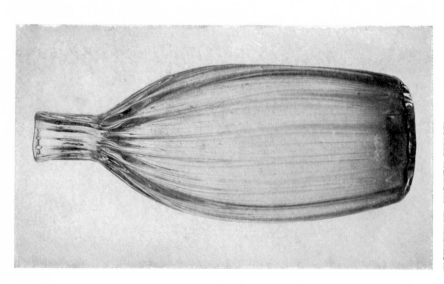

EIGHTEENTH CENTURY STIEGEL

MASONIC BOTTLE WITH CLASPED HANDS, THE STARS
REPRESENTING STATES OF THE UNION

AN EARLY BOTTLE SHOWING SHEARED NECK.  TREE DECORATION

THE JACKSON BOTTLE IS CONSIDERED A VALUABLE SPECIMEN
BELONGING TO THE "STORMY THIRTIES"

EARLY MOSES BOTTLE

FISH BOTTLE

bottles came into use; some of them tiny flasks, so small that they would fit snugly into one's pocket or glove. These ranged from one and a half to three inches in length, displaying great beauty as well as grace of line and delicate workmanship. Many of the existing specimens are exquisite in coloring, particularly those decorated with colored glass ribbons which run up and down the sides.

Such bottles stare out at us from the shelf of an ardent collector of American glass rarities, some of them take the form of a tiny glass sea horse; others are shaped like a gourd. It was one of the latter that was inherited from my great-grandmother—a quaint little bottle which had been presented to her as a wedding gift. This was discovered in an old hair trunk under the eaves of the attic, together with a camel's hair shawl and several rolls of India silk brought over seas in a clipper ship during the days of commercial prosperity. My great aunt, who had inherited it, remembered the little gourd flask as one filled with salts and carried in a gorgeous bead bag that swung from great-grandmother's arm when she went to church. It seemed to liven her spirits during the long tedious sermon which often lasted over an hour.

From Cape Cod to Virginia, from the cornfields of Indiana to the island of Manhattan, all along the wayside are farmhouses and homes in which are treasured many an odd bottle, though often enough the owner knows little and cares less concerning its history or significance. Yet these may by chance prove to be rare examples of the early glass blower's art, valuable acquisitions to any collection.

# WINDOWS

## Chapter Eight

ACCUSTOMED as we are to houses flooded with light and sunshine, it is difficult to realize that window glass as we know it was not in general use until the eighteenth century. We take our windows as a matter of course, not stopping to think that once they were regarded as such luxuries that when the Duke of Northumberland was leaving his estate he was advised by his steward to order his windows taken out and stored for safe keeping until his return. Shortly after our own Revolutionary War, there was to be found in Paris, that center of the world's civilization, a flourishing establishment for the making of window sashes *fitted with oiled paper!* Indeed, as recently as 1918 both France and Belgium resorted to this method of enclosing their houses, all window glass factories being destroyed or unable to carry on business.

The old Romans made extensive use of mica, shells, and alabaster for windows, and were only beginning to adapt glass to this purpose when the barbarian rush from the north put an untimely end to arts and industries, and scattered the skilled workmen to other parts of the world. Such examples as are found in the Pompeian ruins and in various parts of London show this Roman window glass to have been at least half an inch thick, in small pieces, evidently made by the casting process, in which the melted material was poured on a flat stone or similar surface and smoothed out as well as might be with the crude tools available. Such a thing as a sheet of perfectly clear glass of any considerable size was unheard of in those days.

Whether the first glass houses in America turned out window glass, or whether this article was entirely imported from the mother country prior to the eighteenth century, we cannot be sure, since authorities differ on this point. Some claim that experiments were made in that earliest furnace built near Jamestown about 1608, and again in the plant at Salem, Massachusetts, in 1639. Be that as it may, we are reasonably sure that it was made in Allowaystown, New Jersey, in 1739, and that the production was carried on for over forty years, although a venture made by Robert Hewes in Concord, New Hampshire ended in failure, as did other attempts undertaken by ambitious glass makers in various locations.

The unceasing competition of foreign glass, the lack of skilled workmen, inadequate equipment, and the heavy cost of transporting raw materials and the finished product all combined to create an impossible handicap for the struggling young industry. But in 1792 the Boston Crown Glass Company, chartered in 1787, began opera-

A THIRTY-PANED SEVENTEENTH CENTURY WINDOW IN THE
JOHN S. LAWRENCE HOUSE AT TOPSFIELD, MASS.

SMALL PANED WINDOWS IN GARRISON HOUSE,
NEWBURY, MASS., BUILT IN 1666

tions and won the distinction of being the first American establishment after Wistar to produce window glass at a profit. Several factors contributed to their success. Heretofore the use of wood as fuel had necessitated continual moving; the substitution of coal made it possible to develop the industry in one place. Moreover, the legislature, at last awake to its duty and its opportunity, gave liberal assistance. Thanks to its broad minded policy the Company was exempt from taxation, was given for fifteen years the exclusive right to manufacture window glass in Massachusetts, and its workmen were released from military service. Thus protected, the business prospered, and the quality of its output was said to be superior to that of the imported article.

Of no less value than the foregoing benefits were the improved methods of manufacture. The old casting process could never be profitable, either from the point of view of quantity or quality, and it was not until the blowing process came into use that real window glass was made.

In the crown glass method a large mass of melted glass was gathered on the end of a blow pipe and blown into a hollow sphere. The pontil iron or "punty," tipped with melted glass, was then attached to the opposite side of the sphere and the blow pipe was removed. This left a hole, so that the glass formed a sort of bowl or globe, not unlike the gold fish globes of the present day in shape. The globe was then softened by exposing it to an intense heat, with the hollow side toward the furnace, and was whirled until, by the action of centrifugal force, it spread out into a disc, or "table," clinging to the pontil by a knob or boss in the center. When it was quite flat it was removed from the pontil, put into the annealing oven, where it was cooled gradually, to reduce its brittle quality, and then cut into pieces.

Although more practical than the old casting process this method was expensive and wasteful. It is easy to see that it was not possible to make very large sheets or tables of glass by this process, and these had to be cut up into smaller pieces because of the "bull's eye" or lump of glass in the center, by which the table was originally attached to the pontil. These bulls' eyes were used for transoms, sky lights, and other places where transparency was not a requisite, and they are highly valued to-day for the antique appearance they lend; but they were considered almost in the light of waste products in the days when they broke directly into the center of the sheet of glass that was made for use in windows. Moreover, even several inches away from the bull's eye, crown glass is almost certain to have circular marks which mar it in the estimation of any one who does not value them as an evidence of antiquity.

# Windows

Even now one occasionally sees the old bulls' eyes, as in the Stark Mansion in Dumbarton, New Hampshire, where there is a whole sash of them, though ordinarily, as mentioned before, they were used as decoration in side lights and transoms. The Putnam Lodge in Danvers, Massachusetts, shows some of this old glass in its attic windows.

It is interesting to note that the Sandwich Glass Company revived this old bull's eye pattern. Most of this variety of window glass made by this firm was used for panels in doors. Some of it is to be found in the doors of certain houses on Beacon Hill, Boston, while a complete set is treasured in the house which Deming Jarves built for his son.

The so-called "hand-process" of blowing glass in cylindrical form, and then flattening it out, is a step in advance of this old crown glass method. It was practiced as early as the eleventh century and was probably perfected by the Venetians, but it was not in general use until the nineteenth century. It involves tremendous labor, requires a high degree of skill, and produces an inferior article, yet in spite of these drawbacks it was the accepted method of manufacturing window glass until early in the twentieth century. Even now it is commonly used in some parts of the United States, and in many European countries. Meanwhile, after repeated experiments, and

[ 87 ]

the expenditure of large sums of money, the hand process was supplanted by machinery, though the glass continued to be made in cylinders.

For years men attempted to cast glass in sheet form, thus eliminating the flattening process with its labor and waste. Millions of dollars were spent in experimenting; men gave their lives in efforts to solve the problem, but it was not until this century that a sheet glass machine was perfected whereby it became possible to produce a clear, strong, thoroughly satisfactory sheet glass without undue cost in man power and money.

With window glass accounted a luxury in European countries it is not to be supposed that it was viewed otherwise in the colonies. The first windows were probably little more than slits in the crude block houses, in keeping with the simple batten doors. Even oiled paper was not to be had save by the well-to-do and it seems likely that the windows of this early period were merely openings furnished with shutters hung on strips of leather tanned by the colonists themselves, for metal hinges had not yet arrived overseas.

In the second period, when cottages took the place of the block houses to some extent, the windows were larger and more likely to be fitted with tiny leaded panes, a type to which the small pieces of greenish or dark colored glass were well adapted. The cases were simple, finished

without sill or ornamentation of any kind, often only a
foot or so in width and but little higher. They were
fashioned after the English casements of that time,
though it is probable that many of them swung in rather
than out, thus affording greater protection. This casement type still prevails in Denmark, Norway and
Sweden. Some of these windows were imported and
some of native manufacture. They were irregularly
placed on the house walls, with more reference to their
usefulness within than to the effect produced without.
Reproductions of such windows may be seen in the Re-
becca Nourse house in Danvers, Massachusetts, where
the panes are square; in the Paul Revere house, Boston,
which shows diamond shaped panes, and in the Parson
Capen house in Topsfield, Mass.

The panes were tiny, sometimes measuring only three
and a half by five and a half inches. Occasionally a
casing would hold two or three casements. Such windows rarely had shutters but straight lengths of homespun hung on the inside—our first American draperies.
The casements were heavily leaded and the little windows
could not have admitted much light.

This type persisted until about 1700 when it was replaced by the double hung window. During this century
windows began to be regarded somewhat architecturally
and not wholly as utilitarian features. They were placed

more regularly, ornamental trim took the place of the simple casing, paneled shutters were used within, and outside shutters were once more seen, these latter showing cut designs, crescents, half moons, and the like.

Happily for us the leaded window has come into its own again, along with the open fire, the old-time candlesticks, and many other delightful reminders of the days when a house was a home and our grandmothers dispensed hospitality with a sweet graciousness and dignity. What is more attractive than the latticed casement window, or the more elaborate leaded window carrying a simple painted design? The plain leaded sash is used effectively in gable windows, obviating the peculiar staring quality such windows frequently have. Variations, either simple or elaborate, are to be found in halls, on stairways, in libraries, and dining rooms, in fact, there is scarcely a room in the house where such a window cannot be used with good effect.

By the latter part of the eighteenth century the use of glass for windows had become so much an accepted policy, that we find a homestead law requiring at least one in every cabin, and we can picture our pioneer ancestors westward bound each carrying carefully a small four-paned window to be installed in the new home. What would those same pioneers think of the modern home with

BULL'S EYE PANES IN THE WARNER HOUSE,
PORTSMOUTH, N. H., 1723

PIERCE NICHOLS HOUSE, SALEM, MASS., 1782

its windows in every conceivable place, its sun parlors, and its glassed porches?

Among the myriad variations of windows which we have to-day, there are, perhaps, none of more peculiar interest than the sun-purpled panes to be seen in some of the older houses, facing the Common, on Beacon Street, in Boston. Irregularly placed, sometimes an entire row, sometimes a single pane in a sash, they range from faint lilac to deep purple, their delicate amethyst tones challenging the attention of the passer-by, arousing curiosity and usually admiration.

There be folk who regard these strangely colored panes as interlopers, and who wonder why the owners of such beautiful homes tolerate them. The owners, however, cherish them as something infinitely precious and consider themselves fortunate indeed in their possession. For these curiously tinted panes cannot be replaced. Sunlight and time, acting on some element (probably oxide of manganese) used in excess in a batch of glass, have produced this charming result. Seen from the Mall, they are fairy windows, gleaming and glowing in the afternoon sun, glorifying those substantial, dignified houses, and shedding an air of mystery and romance over the Hill.

# TABLE GLASS

STIEGEL BLUE GLASS. DIAMOND PITCHER AND SPIRAL SALT CELLAR

STIEGEL GREEN SUGAR BOWL AND PITCHER

, drinking glasses, and similar things; while the represented utensils for use in kitchen and pantry, as jars for the storage of preserved fruit, and milk , which were used in cooling the milk and in raising m for the making of butter and cheese.

As time went on new patterns in tableware were developed and the range of sizes became larger. We have only recently begun to realize the charm of these early pieces, ut for several years the recognition of their value has been steadily increasing, and old bits of tableware now bring prices that to an outsider seem exorbitant. However, since value depends upon the relation of supply and demand, and since the demand is steadily increasing while the supply of old glass naturally decreases, owing to breakage, rising prices are to be expected.

Happy is the collector who can unearth in the remote corners of an old home a forgotten and neglected stack of glass dishes which, when washed and brought to light, are found to include some of the pieces that every one is looking for. Unfortunately, such finds are becoming more and more rare, and it will not be long before every desirable bit of old glass will be included in some one's collection and duly exhibited with pride by the fortunate possessor.

Numerous pieces of ancient American glass are still treasured in the historic city of Salem, Massachusetts.

ENGRAVED STIEGEL FLIP GLASSES

## Chap

W<small>HILE</small> bottles and wind

only products of the first J

beads for traffic with the India

tempt, it was not long before ou

demanding glass for their tables.

Probably not much glass was u

and most of such pieces as there w

over from the mother land, for duri

our country's settlement these busy

have time to give to the frivolities of

were filled with the work required to

necessities of existence; their tables were

tive food, and the table service was probab

crude as the other details of the pioneer ho

Later, when settlements became better pop

was more leisure to consider decorative effec

doubt our forbears were stimulated to produce

tractive settings by remembrance of the homes

left when they migrated to this country.

Early American glass for household use was ma

tured in two phases; one, for the table, included pit

sugar bowls, salt cellars, cruets, sweetmeat dishes,

plates

other

such

pan

crea

op

r

b

# Table Glass

Many of them were doubtless standing on the shelves of the same gleaming white china cupboards they now adorn when Hawthorne was a familiar guest in the House of the Seven Gables. There are still found many heirlooms in the large colonial houses of the early eighteenth century period, in the building of which the noted wood carver, Samuel McIntire, took a hand, possibly designing some of the china cupboards which hold these rare bits of glass.

Our second President, John Adams, took a keen interest in American glass, and after his death many pieces were found on the shelves of his corner cupboards, pieces then considered of so little worth that they were practically sold for a song. There is still treasured in a New England household a set of pressed table glass that was used by the children and grandchildren of the President, and sold after his death. It consists of a small pitcher, sugar bowl, etc.; about a dozen pieces in all.

Bowls were a favorite output of the early glass houses and now eagerly sought after. They were made in all sizes from tiny ones, the size of a teacup, to great ones holding a gallon or more. Some were shaped much like hats, with flat-topped crowns turned downward and broad brims such as were worn by Quakers. The Wistars designed many of this type in the green glass for which the Wistar factories were noted. Others were made by the

Chelmsford Glass Company of Pembroke, New Hampshire, and in other glass factories at various times. These bowls served a double purpose, being used for the table as well as for the pantry.

Stiegel early realized the necessity for tableware, and entered the field, designing a variety of pieces. Especially noteworthy are his sugar bowls and pitchers. These were frequently short and bulgy, the bowls ornamented with a knob or pointed top on the cover, and the pitchers with a flaring lip. Prominent among the pieces of table glass turned out by Stiegel were fruit dishes of blown glass depicting grape decoration ground on the sides.

Some delightful sugar bowls and cream pitchers from various unidentified glass houses were made in three section contact molds, following the conventional patterns used in that process, such as the sunburst with ribbing, both vertical and horizontal. An interesting pair of this ware, blown by Matt Johnson at Stoddard, New Hampshire, lately came into the market, sold by the owners, Edwin and Crist O'Neil, who verify their antiquity.

The New England Glass Works originated many interesting types of fluted overlaid bowls, which occasionally show a six sided base. Most of these were clear flint, though some were made in blue, green, purple and opalescent white with a blue base.

# Table Glass

Among the various bits of table glass, no single class offers greater variety than salt cellars. Stiegel made them in many shapes, often with the bowl in form suggestive of a tulip and with bases generally smaller than the widest flare of the bowl. These were made in colors, as well as clear flint, the most desired ones being in the best shade of Stiegel blue. In many of them the pattern was impressed in condensed form upon the parison of metal by the use of a pattern mold, after which the bit was blown to full size, leaving that softness of outline and detail, that effect of waves, or rather wavelets, that this process produces in greatest perfection. Some of these little salt cellars of Stiegel's are quite crooked, illustrating very well Hunter's statement that "measured by the forceps, these handblown pieces are all asymmetrical, measured by the subtler micrometer of our responsiveness to vitality and beauty, many of them approach perfection."

The Sandwich salts have an even wider range of color and shape. They are found in clear flint, in green, blue, and many shades of brown and amber. The shapes are in infinite variety, and show more angular outlines than the blown pieces of Stiegel and other earlier glass makers. This is quite to be expected, because in pressing glass it is possible to achieve sharper outlines than in blowing it.

and rectangular shapes are as easy to make as round or oval.

A little boat-shaped salt cellar is generally accepted as the earliest of the Sandwich salts. This has the imprint "B. & S. Glass Co." on the stern; "Sandwich" on the bottom, and "Lafayet" on each of the side wheels. If only the Sandwich works had continued the practice of marking all their pieces there would be less discussion now about the probable source of some bits of glass claimed as Sandwich.

Practically all the early glass houses made salts, and any one who starts a collection of these little dishes need never fear to find it monotonous.

There is a pair of salt cellars treasured in my own family, a part of the American glass in my great-grandfather's house at Newburyport, Massachusetts. When the fire of 1812 swept through the city, taking in its train many of the finest residential mansions, grandfather's old colonial house went up in flames, destroying without remorse the many master craftsmen pieces, the old china as well as the glass. Two rare bits were rescued by a darky mammy who, throwing her shawl over her head for protection, tucked a wonderful colonial mirror under one arm and stowed the pair of salt cellars in her basket.

The glass works at Stoddard, New Hampshire, made

SANDWICH GLASS SALT CELLARS

LATE EIGHTEENTH CENTURY SALT CELLAR

SUGAR SIFTER IN PETAL DESIGN.  SANDWICH GLASS

some interesting compote jars for holding jam, and finished with a glass ball instead of a cover.

These glass balls were made in all sizes from tiny ones about as large as a common marble, for the little creamers, to great ones a foot in diameter, for the large bowls. When they were as large as this, and designed for use as covers, they were often flattened on the bottom so that they would not extend down into the bowl too far. It has been questioned whether quick silver was ever blown into balls for covers, especially those which came from the Zanesville, Ohio, glass works. Quick silver was blown inside hollow candlesticks, rosettes, and vases made in the eastern part of Ohio and in Pennsylvania, therefore we feel sure it must have been employed. These interesting glass balls were put to other uses than the covering of bowls, and some of these uses are mentioned in the chapter on Miscellaneous Glass.

A great variety of tableware was made at the Sandwich works and at the New England Glass Company's factory. Among the most desirable of the Sandwich pieces, from the collector's point of view, are the compotes with waterfall base. These are very rare, and fortunate is he who owns one. There are also deep oval dishes with grooved corners, made probably about 1839, and considered by experts to be among the finest ever produced in this factory.

Sugar bowls and creamers were made in the Sandwich works of clear flint, blue, opalescent and purple glass, also bowls with covers and sweet-meat jars which are used to-day for sugar. Small concave dishes sometimes do service as holders of jam or honey, but they are rarely found now as each year the collecting of glass comes more and more to the fore, and the old bits are being gathered in for private and public collections, until those who formerly were unaware of their value are now on the look-out to obtain the highest prices for their heirlooms.

The workmen at the Saratoga Glass Works made some quite exquisite pieces of table glass for their own use, in the fine green metal used at that factory for the making of bottles. These pieces are very scarce but they are well worth hunting for and the cups, mugs and tapering pitchers that are now and then obtainable are effective either in groups or as single pieces.

Round milk pans, generally green in color, with broad flaring rims and a slightly depressed lip, are now considered so charming that one sees them displayed on sideboards or on the shelves or corner cupboards, where they add their beauty of color and grace of line to the decoration of the room.

Castors, once indispensable for table use, then for a time discarded and hidden away in dark corners, are now being brought out to the light and used as ornaments or

in the setting of the table. A historic one is still in existence, but whether English or American we do not know.
It belonged to John Hancock, whose magnificent house
on Beacon Street, Boston, is now a memory only. Another castor was presented to Marcus Daniels upon his
silver wedding anniversary, in 1870, probably of American manufacture. Both are treasured for sentiment's
sake.

Another historic piece of tableware comes to mind, a
plain little petaled egg glass, probably made at the Sandwich Glass factory. It was the property of the poet
Whittier, who was so fond of it that he had it placed on
his breakfast table every morning.

While we shall probably never be able to accumulate
enough of the old American glass to use it in actual service of the table, some collectors are endeavoring to accumulate a sufficient quantity for use on special occasions.
However, it seems as though one could hardly enjoy eating from anything so precious and so fragile, and most
of us would consider it wiser to set our tables with good
modern glass and keep the treasured old bits to deck our
sideboards or corner cupboards.

# THE FASHION OF CUP PLATES

## Chapter Ten

AMONG the many forms of American glass, perhaps none has a stronger appeal than cup plates unless we give the palm to bottles. Bottles to be sure have been sought eagerly, pursued to their dusty resting places in eaves and cellars, and "written up" by enthusiasts all over the country. In the last analysis, however, they make their strongest appeal to the masculine mind, and their nearest competitors in popularity, the cup plates, find their place in the feminine heart. For what woman does not love a tea party and what is more suggestive of such delightful gatherings than the tiny glass cup plates of our grandmothers' day?

What pictures these little plates bring up, of stately old-time ladies in voluminous frocks of prunella and silk, of dainty tables, gate-legged or dish-top, laid with the finest of homespun napery, with sprigged china, or perchance pink luster, and slender silver spoons, tables which held rich plum cake and crisp cookies, golden preserves, and toothsome ginger brought from far lands in squat blue jars—and the teapot, of course, slender and graceful, round and fatsome, of gleaming silver, mellow pewter, or egg-shell china, as the case might be.

In cool weather the table would be set by the crackling fire, with perhaps a silken screen to protect one from the blaze. On summer days the arbor was the appointed place, with climbing vines and gay flowers nodding over the trellis. But whatever the setting, the cup that cheers was the beginning and the end.

Inevitable as the cup was the little cup plate for the protection of shining cloth or polished mahogany. For in those days Fashion decreed that cups should be without handles, and it was well-nigh impossible to hold the small hot bowls; so the tea was poured into the deep saucers and the cup set in the miniature plate.

Long ago this quaint old custom was cast into the discard and for years the cup plates were consigned to utter obscurity; relegated to top shelves, dark cupboards, or given to children to play with. But of recent years glass has come into its own again and the cup plate has been brought forth into the light of day. Such searching of closets and garrets, such scanning of patterns, such frantic questionings as to "Where *could* they have gone? I *know* we had some!" Such triumphant swagger when the lost is found.

Tea was practically unknown in New England before 1700. Our Puritan forefathers drank thin gruel, cider, sangaree, or water; New England rum as well, for they were not teetotalers in those days!

# The Fashion of Cup Plates

The first American tea drinking, as far as we know, was held in Ipswich, Massachusetts, in 1739. The gentle-women of the town, descendants of old English families, were eager to establish the old custom in the new land. Social affairs were none too numerous and the practice of "afternoon tea" spread apace throughout all New England, the initial gatherings being unique in that each guest brought her own cup and saucer, spoon and cup plate. Tradition has it that more than one conservative husband remonstrated at the popular parties which they regarded as vain extravagrance, demanding as they did the purchase of a tea service, costing from thirty shillings to as many pounds.

Salem received her first tea through Elias Hasket Derby, famous as the man who opened trade with China. His ship, the *Grand Turk*, under command of Ebenezer West left port in November, 1785, carrying home products to Canton. She returned heavily laden with tea, silks and nankeen, the forerunner of a long and illustrious line of merchantmen which carried the Stars and Stripes to the far ports of the Orient, and brought honor to Salem and her shipmasters.

For all lovers of the old and romantic, the little cup plates of glass and china have a peculiar appeal. Perhaps because they were so intimate a part of the home life of our forefathers. When all is said and done, the hospitable board is the center of family life and around it cling our most cherished memories. There is a deal of truth in the old Chinese saying that it is good for a man to get back to his own tea cup.

Whatever the cause, cup plates are eagerly sought after and have become the object of many a collector's enthusiasm. The earliest ones were of china, many of them of the familiar dark blue ware that we know as Staffordshire. Later, as glass tableware became increasingly popular, we find glass cup plates appearing everywhere. They were made in English and Irish factories for importation and sale in this country, but there were also many of American make.

The Boston and Sandwich Glass Company probably led the way, but their example was speedily followed by almost every glass factory until the country was fairly flooded with cup plates of native manufacture. The early specimens, like most of the American glass of that period, were crude, rather heavy, and of poor color. Constant experiments, however, with attendant improvements in methods, resulted in a clear, brilliant glass, that of the Sandwich plant being distinguished by a beautiful silvery luster. From an old workman we learn that a man and a boy could make 1600 of these little plates in a day, an achievement impossible before the invention of pressed glass. Some of these pressed plates show lacy

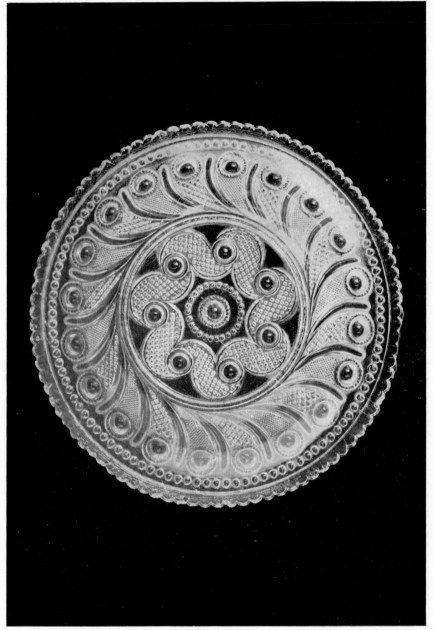

SANDWICH GLASS CUP PLATE, PEACOCK FEATHER DESIGN

SANDWICH GLASS CUP PLATES. 1, BUTTERFLY AND FLOWER DESIGNS;
2. SCALLOPED EDGE WITH STAR DECORATION

SANDWICH GLASS CUP PLATES

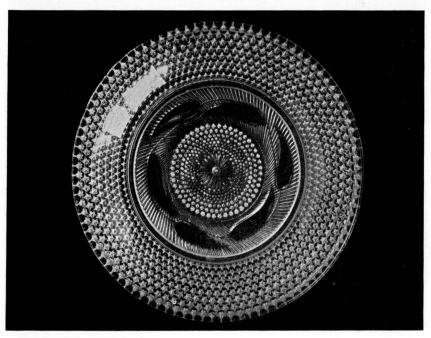

SANDWICH GLASS CUP PLATE

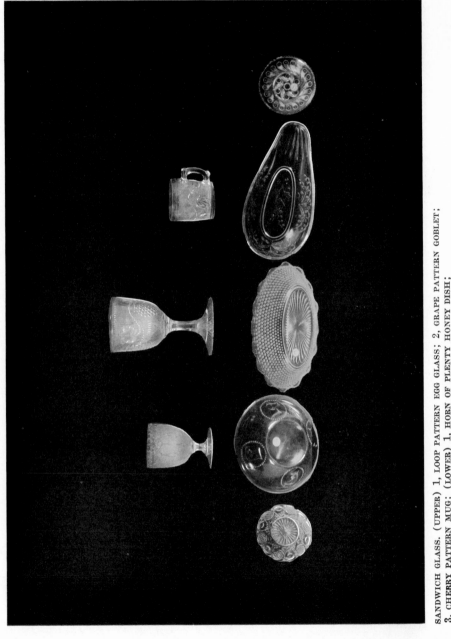

SANDWICH GLASS. (UPPER) 1, LOOP PATTERN EGG GLASS; 2, GRAPE PATTERN GOBLET; 3, CHERRY PATTERN MUG; (LOWER) 1, HORN OF PLENTY HONEY DISH; 2, HORSE'S HEAD SAUCE DISH; 3, GENERAL GRANT PATTERN; 4, LILY OF THE VALLEY PATTERN; 5, PEACOCK PATTERN HONEY DISH

patterns, others were decorated with stars or rosettes in amber, blue and white, though the colored plates were more costly and were never considered to be in as good taste as those of clear glass.

The first ones taken from the new mold were sharp and clear in outline. As the molds became worn through constant use the outlines were softer and more blurred. This fact has aroused more or less discussion among collectors, some claiming that the latter are more valuable, an opinion open to question.

While many of the conventional designs are attractive, the keenest interest attaches to those cup plates which reflect the historic and political events of their time. Of these none was more productive of a variety of designs than the lively Harrison presidential campaign, known as the "Log Cabin Campaign" and memorable for the slogan "Tippecanoe and Tyler too." In the so-called Log Cabin series are the Fort Meigs Log Cabin, the Log Cabin with Cider Barrel, Tree and Flag, the Log Cabin with Flag, and the Log Cabin with Chimney and Cider Barrel. This latter shows a somewhat more hospitable cabin than the others, with a generous homey outside chimney on one end and the inevitable cider barrel beneath the window. The Fort Meigs is the only one of the series which carries any lettering. At the top, in the border itself, is the word "Tippecanoe," the nickname earned by Harrison in his defeat of Tecumseh. In the center of the plate, directly above the cabin appears the name "Fort Meigs," reminiscent of the War of 1812, and in the lower border is printed "W. H. Harrison." The Log Cabin with the Flag is a very small plate and exceedingly rare.

Closely associated with these plates are the Harrison cup plates, bearing the profile of Harrison. Above the portrait are the words "Maj. Gen. W. H. Harrison"; and below, "Born Feb. 9, 1773." Most of these plates have the word "President" in the upper border and the date "1841" in the lower border, but occasionally one sees a plate without this border lettering.

The Beehive is another characteristic Harrison emblem, and the prettiest plate of them all. It has a scalloped edge, and a charming border of laurel leaves encircling a beehive and nine bees. This recalls the Sandwich pattern used on larger plates commonly known as the "Strawberry and Thistle" pattern, but which proves on close examination to picture, not berries at all, but beehives! This design even found its way into the table linen made in the year 1841.

The American eagle has ever been a favorite design in the plastic arts, as well as in painting. As we often wonder idly whether any one ever counted all the lions in Venice, so we might speculate on the number of eagles in some of our American cities. One of the older ones is still to be seen on the barn of the fine Pierce-Johonnot-Nichols estate in Salem, Massachusetts, while another proudly surmounts the Custom House in the same old city; the Custom House made forever memorable by Nathaniel Hawthorne, who found time in the intervals of his work as surveyor of the port, to write "The Scarlet Letter."

It was therefore but natural that the eagle should find himself duly impressed upon the popular cup plate and there are said to be no less than ten different examples of this design. There are large eagles and small eagles, some bordered with the old Greek motive of the Egg and the Dart, others showing stars, some with shells on a stippled ground. Sometimes the noble bird holds in his talons crossed laurel leaves with arrows. Commemorative of the settlement of the boundary between Canada and the United States is the one showing a flower border with trees, presumably pines, at the bottom. This specimen has four stars and is dated 1831, and is more common than many of the others.

One of the most attractive designs, as well as one of the rarest, is a very small plate of clear glass, with edge of dotted scallops and thirteen stars in the center with an eagle. The stars, indicating of course the thirteen original colonies, figure also in two eagle plates showing the sunburst design, as well as in another rare example, with a scalloped edge and an inner border of conventionalized daisies, rosettes, etc.

Then there is the Fort Pitt plate with its lovely peacock border, its finely done eagle with his scroll bearing the words "Fort Pitt," and its twenty-four stars, indicating that the plate was made between 1821 and 1836, the respective dates of the admission to the Union of Missouri and Arkansas. This plate appears in two styles, one having a scalloped edge, the other plain. Another rare eagle plate is the Hop or Blackberry-Vine, so named from the encircling vine.

The Grapevine and the Fleur-de-Lis give their names to two charming plates. Both are comparatively rare in their class. The former has a lacelike edge of alternate points and scallops and a diminutive eagle within a circle of dots. The latter shows an edge of regular scallops, a wide border of fleur-de-lis and a somewhat conventional flower form, within which is another circle of smaller flowers. Then there is an eagle plate of somewhat less distinction, with plain edge and conventional border of scrolls or arabesques.

Bunker Hill Monument, Mecca of American tourists, provides the central figure in four familiar designs, each differing slightly from the others. Two have draped borders, while the others show braids. One of the latter

has thirteen stars, the other but twelve. One of the
draped border plates has twelve stars, the other has none.
All four have scalloped edges and all have lettering, this
latter differing somewhat though each one has the words,
"Bunker Hill Battle Fought June 17, 1775." To this
plain statement of fact the smaller of the braided border
plates adds, "From the Fair to the Brave." The draped
border plates go still farther and add to the above, "Cor-
nerstone Laid by Lafayette June 17, 1825. Finished by
the Ladies." This last statement refers to the fact that
the women completed the fund for building the monument. As these plates commemorate an event in the history of Massachusetts it seems fair to suppose that they
were made in Sandwich.

To-day, when ships are increasingly popular as designs, for everything under the sun from tape measures
to stained glass windows, exceptional interest attaches
to the cup plates honoring events in our naval or commercial history. One of the earliest shows the *Cadmus*,
a merchantman transformed into a whaler, and sometimes erroneously called the *Mayflower*. To the *Cadmus*
belongs the distinction of bringing Lafayette to America
in 1824. The plate is somewhat similar in general design to the Grapevine Eagle, though without the lacy
effect of the latter. The edge is of alternating rounded
and pointed scallops, while the central figure, the *Cadmus*

in full sail, is encircled by dots. Both inner and outer borders show scrolls, the former having also shields and stars.

A variant of this plate has a slightly different edge. The *Chancellor Livingston*, a side-wheeler plying between New York and Providence in the early part of the nineteenth century, was named for Robert Livingston. It appears in three plates of slightly different forms, each bearing the name of the boat and each looking curiously like a sailing vessel, for steam was more or less an unknown quantity in those days and captains hesitated to cut loose from all rigging. Similar to these plates is the one bearing the picture of the *Benjamin Franklin*, another early side-wheeler, named for the brilliant statesman. The stippled border shows a design of scrolls, stars and anchors, surmounted by the American eagle holding his shield. The boat flies no less than three flags, the Stars and Stripes, a pennant, and another marked B. F., a fine example of impartiality!

Although the *Maid of the Mist* has given her name to a cup plate the little boat itself is almost overwhelmed by the Falls and the Suspension Bridge. A fifteenth century sun looks down upon the scene and a curiously crude border encircles the whole picture. The edge is plain, and the plate the least attractive of its class, yet its rarity gives it a value otherwise undeserved.

The real aristocrats of the cup plate world are the three of octagonal shape, the "Washington," the "Frigate Constitution," and the "Steamboat, Robert Fulton." Among these the Washington is easily first, not only because of its rarity but by reason of the excellence of the portrait and the exceptional workmanship. A sunburst set in a stippled circle provides an effective background for the rarely fine head. Encircling this inner circle is a laurel wreath and outside this is a flower border and scalloped edge. The Constitution, of course, honors *Old Ironsides*, beloved as the conqueror of the *Guerriere*, under the doughty Isaac Hull. This plate was probably produced at the time funds were raised for rescuing the old boat from demolition. The Robert Fulton differs from the other steamboat plates in not showing any sails.

If an octagonal Washington is the secret goal of all cup plate collectors, the so-called Large Henry Clay runs it a close second. It is a beautiful plate, nearly three inches and a half in diameter, with wide stippled border showing fleur-de-lis and a regular scalloped edge. The finely executed portrait is surmounted by the name of Henry Clay, to whom, however, it bears no resemblance, while below it are acorns, oak leaves, and a spray of laurel. It is a fine example of the glass maker's art, with a wealth of detail not usually found in cup plates, and is not to be confused with the more familiar Clay plates, of which there are six variants, all showing a border of cornucopias and double-topped shields.

Ranking with the fine Clay and the Washington is the Ringold plate, commemorating the death of Major Samuel Ringold at Palo Alto. The head is an exceptionally delicate piece of work, as are the details of the stock, epaulets, and military collar. These three notable cup plates have never been satisfactorily attributed to any particular glass factory. Lovers of Sandwich like to think that they were produced there, but this seems unlikely as they are so much superior to other portraits known to have been made there. Since the Ringold bottle is known to have come from the Dyottville Glass Works of Kensington, Philadelphia, it seems not unreasonable to think that the Ringold plate may have come from there also.

Of cup plates there is seemingly no end, the most romantic among them being the so-called Heart Series, including innumerable varieties of a sentimental nature. These were often used as gifts between lovers. There are single hearts and double hearts, hearts pierced with arrows, and borders of hearts alternating with sheafs of wheat. The valentine plates are sometimes stamped with eight large stippled hearts, a double line reaching from border to central design, the latter being formed of four rosettes.

# The Fashion of Cup Plates

Floral patterns show the narcissus and the butterfly, the rose and the pansy, with border of pointed leaves. Then there are the grape and the dew-drop, the pineapple, and, of less delicate beauty, the hound, and the steam coach. More or less familiar is the conventional design showing a Maltese cross effect in the center.

A complete collection of these little plates would practically constitute a pictorial record of one period of American history, so linked are the patterns with historic and political events, and with the prevailing fashions.

# DECANTERS, STEM WARE
# AND TUMBLERS

# Chapter Eleven

THE dancing light from the ten foot logs blazing inside the fireplaces in baronial halls of Merry England played over the drinking glasses filled with ruby wine, making pools of brilliant color on the snowy cloth. We in our country are but carrying on the same idea when we place on our table or sideboard tumblers, wine and flip glasses, filling them not with wine as in former days, but with rosy jelly or perhaps a *potpourri* of rose leaves to perfume the air. Or perhaps we set a rare old tumbler of blue glass on the window shelf where it catches the rays of the sun, disclosing tints a thousand times more beautiful than when it stood formerly upon our tables filled with old Burgundy.

On the shelves inside the tap room of the old time ordinary in this country, a tempting array of drinking glasses and mugs often stood. Doubtless among them may have been included an old glass jug of dull green tone, which was sometimes filled with flip and sent to the drinker piping hot, and again held foaming ale, a popular drink of the colonists.

Before decanters came into fashion, the wine was

probably brought to the table in the well known big bellied black bottle, with the imprint on the seal telling the date of the vintage. Later it was poured into decanters which stood gleaming on the sideboard, always ready to be poured into the waiting glasses. The first decanters were simple in form, later they were globular in shape with an engraved festoon, a fashion that lasted only a short time. Still later specimens displayed both initials and emblems, one on either side. Sometimes the emblems represented a trade, such as a shuttle and pair of shears, for a weaver who was proud of his work.

Just when the making of decanters began in this country is not on record. We know, however, that Stiegel produced them in beautiful designs, and many choice pieces from this factory are still in existence. He varied the output in color as well as in shape, making them in dark blue, purple, and other colors, bits that reflect the light with gem-like brightness.

From advertisements we learn that Stiegel designed decanters in quarts, pints, and half pints, tumblers in half pints and gills; also syllabub glasses such as carry us back to the old southern gardens where, under shade of the trees, syllabub was served together with delectable cake made from old English recipes.

There are some of his pieces in existence to-day that are well worth notice, such as a clear glass carafe now among the wonderful collection of old American glass in the Metropolitan Museum in New York. There is also a child's decanter made of green transparent glass, and there is a stopper of white ribbed flint glass which lacks a bottle, the latter not yet unearthed. We also find table jugs of white flint displaying a Venetian diamond pattern, pint jugs, opaque white, finished with enameled steeple designs, and wine glasses so exquisitely designed that they have never been excelled, even at the present day. There are also flip glasses, wonderfully engraved.

Stiegel made tumblers with colored designs applied and fused on to the surface. There was a set of miniature tumblers of this sort that stood on a tray. These were not children's toys as might be imagined, but samples to be carried in their packs by salesmen to show to prospective customers.

Honey colored glass was at one time fashionable for drinking sets. Such a set is still to be seen in the Essex Institute at Salem, Massachusetts. This glass was said to suggest sea anemones swimming in clear water.

Wistarberg put out mulberry decanters and glasses of the same coloring. Among the choicest products of the Wistarberg factory was a rare mug of transparent turquoise finished with a graceful handle. This peculiar light shade of blue was a special characteristic of the Wistar glass, in which dark blue such as Stiegel used so much is seldom found. There is also a decanter of clear flint, conical in shape, with a cup for a cover, in the custom at one period. Other glass works designed similar pieces, notably factories at Albany, Baltimore and Pittsburgh.

Some of the old decanters were blown in contact molds; others had the condensed pattern impressed upon the plastic glass and were afterward blown to full size, retaining the pattern in expanded form. Frequently this pattern was in the form of vertical ribbing, which the blower made into spiral decoration by twisting the bottle as it was being blown.

A helpful method of determining whether clear glass is old or modern is comparing its "color" with other pieces or with a white textile. To the inexperienced all apparently colorless glass is "white," though to glass makers it is "clear," and "white" is generally applied to opaque white glass. But within the range of clear glass there are many tints, and old glass is never entirely colorless. If you are in doubt about it, place a bit of old clear glass on a white tablecloth and see if you do not find a slight greenish tinge. Then place next it a piece of the best modern clear glass and see the difference between them. The modern piece will probably be entirely colorless, because modern methods have been able to attain this quality which glass blowers through all the ages have desired, but which until very recent times was never quite attained.

STIEGEL CORDIAL AND WINE GLASSES. NOTE COTTON STEMS

THREE SECTION MOLD DECANTERS

SANDWICH GLASS TUMBLERS, THUMB MARK DECORATION

(Courtesy of the Metropolitan Museum of Art)

STIEGEL WINE GLASS

EIGHTEENTH CENTURY STIEGEL WINE GLASS

# Decanters and Glasses

At the Sandwich factory tumblers were among the first productions, and the first pressed glass tumbler made was treasured for many years. Afterward it was given away and was sent to the Centennial celebration, where it was accidentally broken.

Rummers were a type of heavy goblet that prevailed during the stage coach era. Many of the shapes at that period were copied from our English ancestors who held noisy revels in the tap room, and required strong, heavy glasses, the more delicate wine glasses being reserved for private use.

Among the decanters made by unknown factories in the three mold-glass, are some small ones, holding about a pint. These are in the sunburst and quilted pattern so often used in this process of molding, and have ball stoppers. They are quite rare and very highly valued. Other larger ones with the same pattern are not so rare as the smaller ones. Decanters in the three mold sunburst and quilted pattern were made at Stoddard, New Hampshire, but these are more interesting than beautiful, being crude and heavy and made of coarse green glass. Many drinking glasses were made in three mold design, among them being flip glasses, barrel shaped tumblers, wine glasses and covered rummers.

There is no type of glass designing that offers more opportunity to the expert glass blower than stem ware.

Wine glasses can be turned out in such a variety of exquisite shapes and with such delicacy of ornamentation that they are in truth a species of *bijouterie*, lacking the more spectacular appeal of the large pieces, but fascinating to any one who loves the fine points of expert workmanship. There is not space here to go into the technicalities of stem ware, which would make a book by themselves, but any one who cares to make a specialty of this branch of collecting will find in American glass a variety as rich and a technique as well developed as the best of any other country.

Stiegel, especially, of the early glass makers, turned out wine glasses in great variety and of great beauty. We find in the product of his factory the "cotton" stems and air twists, that mark the best of the English blowing. It is not of course necessary to confine a collection only to the smaller and more delicate pieces of stemware. Sometimes the contrast of fine wine glasses ranged with sturdy rummers or tumblers is more satisfying than when one kind of drinking glass alone is collected. But, whatever the limits of such a collection may be, it is safe to say that nowhere in the field of glass will the collector find the work of the expert craftsman more delicately expressed than in the varied shapes devised for the cup that cheers, and also inebriates, especially in that branch of it known as stem ware.

# LANTERNS

## Chapter Twelve

THERE is perhaps no branch of collecting that offers more charm and variety than lighting devices, and one of the most attractive features about it to many people is the fact that the precious pieces can usually be put to practical use, whether they are ships' lanterns converted into door lights, tiny glass lamps wired for bedside reading or always satisfying candlesticks with their hand molded candles shedding a soft light over the dinner table.

The task of collecting lanterns is one of unfailing interest, for the variations in this type of light are almost endless. Like the bears of Goldilocks, there are big lanterns, little lanterns and middle-sized lanterns. Lanterns of wood, tin, brass, iron, copper and bronze with windows of horn, mica, or glass. Lanterns which burned candles, others which had lamps, the variation in these latter being almost as wide as in the lanterns themselves. Tall lanterns and short lanterns, some with metal bails, others with leather handles; some with short squatty globes like the cheeks of a boy blowing up a paper bag, and others tall and slender with much dignity. Lanterns for the home, the shop, the street, the boat and the train;

and lanterns for use indoors and out. Square lanterns, round lanterns, and lanterns with six sides.

The earliest authoritative record we have of this kind of light is found in the fresco of an Egyptian tomb, showing a soldier carrying a long pole from which is suspended a lantern similar in style to the perforated type common in England and America in the sixteenth and seventeenth centuries, and not unlike the early Chinese lanterns of oiled paper. Probably there was no glass used in this ancient luminary but it was the remote ancestor of the up-to-date lanterns that give warning to the engineer, driving his train through the night, in this modern land of speed, as well as the progenitor in direct line of the arc lights that turn night into day in our cities.

When one considers how much of the world's business is carried on after dark it seems incredible that progress in street lighting should have lagged as it certainly did.

Searching the records for the first American ancestor of our modern street light, we find a huge iron basket atop of a pole erected on the highest hill in Boston Town. Filled with pine knots, it was lighted in times of emergency as a signal to the surrounding towns that some mischief was on foot. Hence the name Beacon Hill. Later, following the French custom of a much earlier date, similar baskets, smaller in size, were put on the corners of the most frequented streets, to be lighted by the watchman;

HAND LANTERNS WITH WHALE OIL LAMPS

thus lightening his task in more ways than one, as he trudged on his nightly rounds, swinging his own little lantern and calling out his deep "All's well!"

These watchmen's lanterns form a class by themselves, within which they show considerable variety. The earliest type was probably the small dark tin lantern with a mica front. Then there were triangular lanterns, some measuring not more than four inches in height, with two wooden sides and a front of glass, or with two sides of glass and a tin back which let down to give access to the tiny three cornered lamp within. A later style was the bull's eye, with its curved door of heavy glass which could be covered by a tin slide controlled by a knob at the bottom. These were in various sizes and usually burned sperm oil, some having two wicks, others but one. Most of this class of lanterns were provided with bails for easy carrying, but one curious little light, evidently intended for indoors and said to have been used in the United States Treasury Department, is in two pieces, the lower part looking much like a round box with a D-shaped handle, the ventilated top fitting down on this. Another type for inside use has a pear-shaped glass globe with perforated metal top and base. This type, too, was used in the Treasury Department.

In 1772, three years before Paul Revere was to hang his famous lantern from the steeple of Christ Church,

a meeting was held to discuss the advisability of lighting the streets of Boston. Considering that said streets
were even more narrow and crooked than they are to-day,
it would seem that such action was not out of place.
Meetings do not always have results, but this one did,
for a committee was appointed, of which John Hancock
was a member, to order from England several hundred
lanterns, or in the words of the record "lamps suitable for
properly lighting ye streets and lanes of this town."
These were to be paid for by subscription. But the lanterns were not to be had too easily, for the brig *Loring*
which brought them, in addition to a cargo of tea, was
driven ashore on Cape Cod, and we read in a letter written
by John Andrew in 1773: "It is unlucky that ye *Loring*
has ye lamps on board for our streets. I am sorry if they
are lost, as we shall be deprived of their benefit in consequence of it this winter."

However the metal frames of the lamps seem to have
been salvaged and one Thomas Newell was engaged to
fit sides for them. Beginning March 2, 1774, they were
hung, their exact locations being fixed by two responsible
persons chosen from each ward for this purpose. While
no recorded description of these first street lights has been
found, it is assumed that they were small framed tin lanterns, suspended from iron cranes placed at the corners
of the busiest thoroughfares.

# Lanterns

Ships' lanterns are as interesting and as varied as those carried by the watchmen. From the U. S. S. *Enterprise*, in service in the War of 1812, came a tall, round, copper lantern with a horn window, burning a candle, and having a D-shaped handle. This must have belonged to a much earlier period.

In Dickens' "American Notes" is an amusing description of the diminutive steamboat on which he went from Springfield to Hartford in 1842, a boat so small that Dickens suggests it may have been half-pony power. This tiny craft carried in its cabin a lantern with a heavy glass cylinder, a perforated top fitted with a large ring, and a whale oil lamp, the whole fastened securely to the wall with a strip of brass.

Another river boat, the *Oliver Ellsworth*, plying between Hartford and New York in 1829, had a somewhat more elaborate lantern, semi-circular in shape, its top and back of pierced tin, its straight front of glass. This lantern had a single-burner, whale oil lamp of copper, the light of which was somewhat increased by the silver plated lining of the frame.

Other lanterns in this class were of the bull's eye pattern, their heavy glass set in a projecting tube. Some of these had copper lamps, burning lard oil, and were provided with stout brass bails.

A somewhat earlier type of ships' lantern is to be seen

in the Peabody Museum, Salem, Massachusetts. This is a clumsy wooden model, about two feet high, its glass panels held in place by strips of wood. It burned a candle instead of a lamp. This veteran was used by Captain Samuel Page of Danvers, Massachusetts, some time previous to 1750.

More elaborate than any of the foregoing is a lantern which came from the ill-fated *Caleb Cushing*, sunk by the Confederates in 1863 off Cape Elizabeth. This light has French ruby glass set in heavy copper fittings with steel bands. It has a whale oil lamp of copper with a half wick.

It is quite possible to pick up starboard and port lights in the antique shops to-day. In some of these the heavy tops turn back on a hinge to permit of putting the candle in place.

Of entirely different character is the light which hangs above the door of the Iron Master's house in Saugus. This is of brass and from its cylindrical body come three straight wick tubes, each having an extra spout beneath to catch the drippings and drain them back into the lamp. It has a dome shaped cover and a bail of generous size. This may have served as a ship's lantern and later have been used in a store.

Railroad lanterns have an interest all their own, though they show less variety than the other types. The earliest

cars, or coaches as they were called in those days—and
they really were like stage coaches linked together—carried upright lanterns on each side, feeble forerunners of
our glaring headlights of to-day. Later the so-called
"Post-Chaise" had a curious little light with three sides
of glass and a whale oil lamp with a single burner. A
polished concave reflector did good service in making the
most of what light there was. At night this lantern was
fastened above the rear seat of the coach, a seat sacred to
the use of ladies.

Conductors' lanterns in the early days were similar to
those in use now. They were usually protected by a wire
guard and provided with a bail of ample size, or occasionally with a rigid metal ring at the base, through
which the conductor could slip his arm, thus retaining full
use of both hands. Many of these old lanterns show the
initials of the road ground into the glass.

Lanterns with definite historical associations are always
interesting, the more so when they are of unusual design,
as the two-story iron one which was brought home as a
trophy from the expedition in 1745 when the little army
of untrained New Englanders, aided by a small fleet of
British vessels, captured Louisberg from the French.

Another historic lantern is the very crude one which
was found in the old brick oven of the house in Torring-
ton, Connecticut, where John Brown, the famous abo-

litionist, was born.   This is an open-faced tin lantern,
semi-circular in shape, the front showing grooves for a
sheet of glass, behind which are three rude sockets for
candles.   There is a handle at the back and ventilation is
secured by a row of holes at top and bottom.   A later
lantern of similar design shows places for four candles;
the handle is at the side and the holes are replaced by
a fluted ventilator at the top.   This style was probably
used to light a shop or shop window.

Most famous is the Hancock lantern from the old
house on Beacon Street in Boston, that house whose
value and significance Boston failed to appreciate until
too late, and the demolition of which is a matter of ever-
lasting regret.   It was built in 1737, a stately stone mansion, within whose hospitable portals many distinguished
guests were entertained, Lafayette, Washington, Lord
Bougainville, and others of equal distinction.   The Hancock lantern, now in the Dr. Quincy Norton collection,
whither it came by inheritance, has an iron frame supporting panels of cathedral glass, and it burns a candle.
Swinging on its slender chains in the upper hall of the
beautiful colonial home, this aristocratic light must have
looked upon many a gay scene in the days when John
Hancock courted Dorothy Quincy, that spirited beauty
who made conquests wherever she went and who led the

handsome young patriot a merry dance before he finally won her for his wife.

As interior lighting came to be looked upon more and more as a necessity, these decorative lanterns were much in demand, many of the larger houses having several both in lower and upper halls, the more elaborate ones imported from France and England. Those of earliest date burned candles but these were gradually superseded by whale oil lamps. The frames were of copper, brass, or bronze, exquisitely wrought; the glass globes, sometimes richly colored, were often beautifully etched or engraved.

Lord Timothy Dexter, that wealthy eccentric of Newburyport, whose handsome and dignified house is still to be seen on High Street (though alas, long since shorn of its fascinating wooden figures), liked plenty of light, and we are told that in his dining room alone were four of these charming lanterns.

# LAMPS

THREE SECTION SANDWICH LAMPS.  CONTACT MOLD
LOOP AND RING PATTERN.  MUSHROOM BASE

PEG LAMPS

MERCURY BLOWN SANDWICH GLASS CANDLESTICKS AND TAPER HOLDER

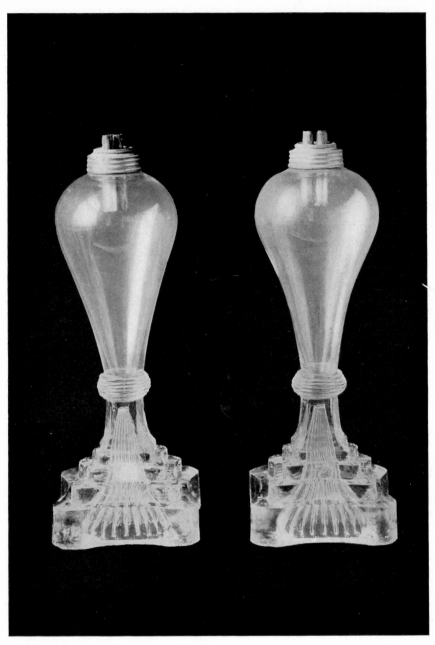

PLAIN FONT LAMPS WITH RIBBED KNOP AND
"NORWICH" BASE WITH INSIDE WATERFALL EFFECT

A COLLECTION OF SANDWICH GLASS LAMPS

SANDWICH GLASS LAMPS. (UPPER) 1, HEART PATTERN; 2, WATERFALL BASE. (LOWER) 1, GOTHIC PATTERN; 2 AND 4, SPARK LAMPS; 3 AND 5, DEEP CUTTING ON BOWL

A LAMP WITH A CUT GLASS
FONT AND BALUSTER STEM

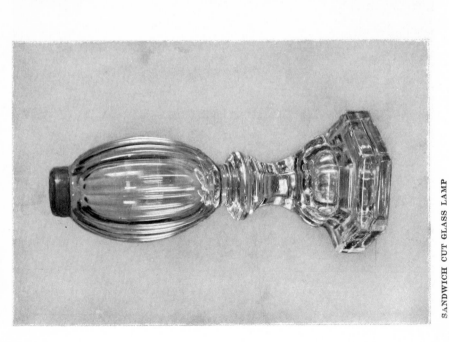

SANDWICH CUT GLASS LAMP

SANDWICH LAMPS. 1 AND 4 HAVE CUT FONTS AND WATERFALL BASES; 2 AND 3 HAVE THE OIL FONTS MOLDED IN PANELS

1, SPARK LAMP; 2, UNUSUAL WAISTED FONT; 3, SPARK LAMP WITH "NORWICH" BASE

## Chapter Thirteen

It is difficult to trace any family resemblance between our modern electric lamp with its clear, steady, brilliant light, and the iron grease lamp of colonial days, with its smoke, its smell, and its feeble flame. Yet the one is the direct descendant of the other, and the genealogical history thereof is a fascinating study.

It takes us back to the beginning of things, far beyond that little old iron lamp of our forefathers, back to the time of the Stone Age. The men of that period used a sandstone lamp almost identical in shape with our American grease lamp, a very shallow saucer or bowl to hold the grease or oil; but, unlike our earliest attempts, these lamps displayed some ornamentation, an ibex or other familiar object etched on the soft stone. This simpler form of lamp persists through the ages, appearing now in this country, now in that, as colonization and civilization spread.

The first lamps in the colonies were undoubtedly brought from the mother country. We are told that Captain John Carver, first governor of Plymouth Colony, purchased an iron "Betty" just before leaving Holland.

This was a shallow dish with a rudely modeled nose on one side, scarcely more than a depression it was, and an equally simple handle on the other. This latter was provided with a hook by which to hang it up, and a chain, on the end of which was a pick or spindle with which to pick the wick, for these early lights were more productive of carbon than of light, and the rag wicks demanded constant cleaning. They remind one of the tiny French cook stoves which require thorough cleaning every day and stoking every half hour. Otherwise within forty minutes you have no fire. So with the "Betty" lamps. Without continual cleaning you have no light, only smoke and smell. The little spindles were not always attached to the lamps. Sometimes the stiletto-like instrument was kept in a little wooden case. Occasionally to-day one of these small receptacles, made of walnut or mahogany, may be seen on an old-fashioned mantel shelf, still holding its slender pick, though the days of its usefulness are long since past.

The "Betty" lamp seems first to have been made for use about a fireplace. In the days of primitive customs the cooking was done over the open fire in heavy iron kettles. The day of white-lined or aluminum ware was far distant. There were no overhead lights. To enable the housewife to see what was going on in her big dark kettle these little lamps were devised. In some of the

# Lamps

English dialects the nickname "Betty" is given to kettles. What more natural than to transfer the name to the handy little light made to use about the fire and the kettles? In such queer and devious ways come many of our well-known expressions—terms which we rarely think to question but the study of which may lead us into fascinating by-paths and to many a curious tale.

The first lamps made in America were probably even more simple than the "Betty," very like their most remote ancestors. One specimen shows a shallow iron saucer with overturned edges which forms four corners, as it were, for the wicks to lie in; no handle of any sort. Another early one resembles a large spoon with the handle bent at right angles to the bowl. This has a hook by which to hang it up.

As early as 1630 bog iron was discovered near Boston, in what is now Saugus, and the thrifty settlers lost no time in setting up a small smelter for making the iron utensils necessary for their simple style of living. Naturally, lamps were numbered among the essentials, and at least one interesting example from this earliest American foundry exists. A clumsy grease lamp in the shape of a cup and saucer, provision in each for a wick, and with a heavy handle connecting the two parts. Aside from its value as a piece of early American craftsmanship, it has the added interest of having been used during the period of the witchcraft delusion in Salem, a somewhat melancholy association. Another lamp to which an equally mournful interest attaches (it was used in Salem jail at about the same time) is also of iron but more like a deep bowl mounted on a rim and with a short downward curving handle.

A rare variant of the open lamp is of dark brown pottery made by the Dutch settlers in Pennsylvania. It has a flat base supporting a two-handled, slightly graduated stand on top of which is a cup or bowl with one lip for the wick. Twisted rags usually formed the wicks for these early lamps.

From time to time changes appeared in the "Betty" lamps. Covers were added, some fitting like the lid of a saucepan, others hinged at the back, some hinged in the middle, still others having a hole in the cover protected by a sliding cap of iron. We are apt to think of the adjustable reading lamp which can be attached to a chair or a bed as a product of twentieth-century ingenuity, but there are specimens of the "Betty" which could be raised or lowered at will.

Since thrift was a cardinal principle in those days, in small matters as well as large, there is often to be seen in the "Betty" a second spout directly below the wick spout. This was to catch the surplus oil from the wick. The "Phœbe" differed from the "Betty" in having a double base, the lower one serving a similar purpose to the drip spout.

But with all these minor improvements and differences in detail, the quality of light remained practically unchanged. It continued to be a case of much smoke and little fire, or a pound's worth of smoke to a pennyworth of light. Then some one conceived the idea of enclosing the wick in a tube—a long step ahead. Lamp bodies were made larger and many were provided with two wicks or even three. Some of the latter resemble little tin cylinders resting on their sides, supported by four very short legs. The wicks are in a line on the top and the lamp is carried by a handle on one end. These were known as guest-room lamps and as an unusual refinement some of them have a shallow spice pan suspended over one of the wicks; the smoke from the burning spice or herbs serving to mitigate somewhat the odor of the burning oil.

Gradually wicks shifted from the side of the lamp to the top, and iron gave way to tin, a neater and more convenient material. Copper and brass were sometimes used and later pewter became very popular. The very crude fish oil was replaced by whale oil, lard oil, and camphene. The latter was highly explosive and required extra long burners to remove the flame as far as possible from the oil. Lard oil wicks were broad and flat as distinguished from the smaller, round wicks of the whale oil burner.

The variety in these old tin lamps is almost bewildering. This applies to all parts of the lamp; the base, the standard, the oil font, and the oil burner. The bases are flat, saucer-like, either deep or shallow conical, or of the familiar petticoat style. The round ones were evidently the most popular but occasionally a square one occurs; very rarely a rectangular oblong one. Standards were also most often round, some tall, some short, some plain, others showing a bit of turning. Handles were commonly placed on the base but sometimes on the standard. The oil fonts were of all sorts and kinds, deep, shallow, round, bell-shaped, flat-sided, as varied as their makers and users.

Early in the eighteenth century, Benjamin Franklin, then a lad in his father's candle shop, impressed with the undue amount of carbon as compared with light from the lamps, experimented and found that two wicks, side by side, not only increased the quantity of light but improved its quality, the stronger current of air consuming more carbon. Following this discovery came the more notable one by Argand, the Swiss chemist, the importance of whose invention of the central draft burner was surpassed only by the accidental discovery of the glass lamp chimney. One of his workmen, holding a bottle too near the flame, broke the bottom, and finding the bottle too hot to hold with comfort, set it down over the flame, which to his amazement at once became steadier and brighter. The significance of this apparently simple thing was not lost upon Argand. Then and there was born the glass chimney, an event which revolutionized lighting and created a new use for glass, a use which was destined to increase the demand for this commodity to undreamed of proportions.

It is interesting to note the various attempts to produce a satisfactory reading lamp. One of the earlier bull's eye type shows a pewter stand similar to a candlestick, but with a drum-shaped oil font having a double wick and a single bull's eye lens. Another, of English make, is known as an improved reading lamp. It is of similar pattern but has two glass bulls' eyes, one on either side of the oil font, each with a tiny pewter shade, evidently designed to make the most of the dim light given by the whale oil burner. Lamps of this kind were in use about the middle of the eighteenth century. It was to be some years yet before glass came into its own as an essential feature of lamps.

Metal lamps, chiefly of tin and pewter, with the Franklin burner, held sway until the first half of the nineteenth century, when the Sandwich Glass Company put out a small attractive glass lamp. It "took" at once and glass lamps became popular almost overnight.

The first ones were very simple, a flaring base, either square or round, supporting a pear-shaped body finished with a brass or pewter collar and cover. The latter screwed on and contained two cylinders for the small whale oil wicks, which reached down into the oil tank. These lamps show the peculiar silvery sheen which distinguished the early Sandwich Glass, a brilliancy due partly to the chemical composition and partly to the method of finishing. This latter known as fire-polishing, consisted of repeated re-heatings of the surface which left it smooth and lustrous.

Glass lamps were made by the New England Glass Co. also, but the products of this factory seem never to have attained the degree of popularity reached by the factory on Cape Cod. By some inexplicable twist of public fancy, Sandwich glass has become famous and the name alone will frequently effect a sale. As it was not common to mark the articles with the firm name, and as the output of both of these factories was large—each employed about five hundred men at the time of their greatest activity—it is not always easy to distinguish with perfect accuracy. It is probable that the Cambridge factory never succeeded in equaling the luster of the early products of the Cape plant.

Another earlier glass factory was located in what is now Quincy, Massachusetts, then known as Germantown.

# Lamps

The lamps made by this firm are known by the shadowy spiral within the stem just below the oil font, a delicate reminder of the gay spirals in glass marbles which delighted our childish hearts.

The Sandwich lamps present an almost endless variety in base, oil font, decoration and color. The oil fonts were evidently of more interest to the designers than were the bases, though these latter show a considerable range of difference. They are round, square, octagonal, flat, fluted, flaring, plain, lined, and molded. The Mushroom and the Step patterns were perhaps the most common, while the Maltese Cross effect is less often seen.

Oil fonts were amazingly varied. Round, oval, urn-shaped, top-shaped; some long and graceful, others short and plump, still others patterned after charming old wine glasses. There were stately table lamps, comfortable go-to-bed lamps. Lamps which look as though they were predestined to shine in drawing-rooms or to achieve literary or historic fame; others, like the little spark lamps, merely humble faithful servants; and hosts of middle class lamps, useful and with a moderate degree of good looks.

The decorations are as diversified as the fonts and bases. There is the always popular "Heart" pattern, the "Cable" developed to honor the laying of the first American cable, the "Hob Nail," the "Thumb Print," the

"Ripple," the "Gothic Window," the "Star and Full Moon" and many others as happily named as these, for to see them is to feel at once that the appropriate name has been given.

Still further possibilities appear in the combinations used, one type of base with many different styles of fonts. Sometimes an American base is combined with an imported body, a bit of work which, by the way, necessitated a high degree of skill. It may have been occasioned by the fact that in the early days of American glass making it was not easy to have the metal collars welded to the body. To get over this difficulty bodies already fitted with collars were imported and put on the native-made base.

Color played an important rôle in this flourishing industry. There are blue lamps and brown lamps; lamps in rich ruby red and in delicate amethyst, in apple green and the myriad shades of amber. Among them all perhaps the most highly prized are those of very deep blue or of canary yellow. Sometimes two colors are used, the one cut out to show the other underneath. With all these countless combinations and variations it seems almost incredible that one so rarely sees an ugly Sandwich lamp. Indeed, it is so unusual as to be inconspicuous.

The "Betty" and the "Phœbe" lamps were found only in metal but there were other types in both glass and metal. Among them are the Sparking lamps, Tavern lamps, Squat lamps, Chamber lamps, and Peg lamps. These terms were more or less interchangeable. The first two are almost identical, the name varying according to where it was used. In public houses it was a Tavern lamp. Used in the home it became a Spark lamp, its tiny glimmer being quite sufficient for lovers, and its going out being the signal for the young man to depart. The name Chamber was applied to this type, as also to the small lamp which swung on a pivot, sometimes known as a Marine lamp. This was particularly useful when the tavern guest found himself a little unsteady on his feet, not quite able to manage a light, perhaps. This little swinging affair kept its upright position despite the uncertain footsteps of its carrier, just as it did aboard ship. Very short dumpy hand lamps were known as Squat lamps. Unlike these others, the Peg lamp has a character of its own. It is somewhat like a top, with no real base but a downward projection designed to fit into a candlestick. These were made in tin, brass, pewter and glass.

A definite historic interest attaches to many of the glass lamps to be seen in some of the present day collections. Among these is the one by whose light much of "Uncle Tom's Cabin" was written. Apart from its literary glory, this lamp is unusual. From its marble base arises a sturdy brass column which supports an octagonal oil font of plain glass. An exceptional pair of lamps came from the home of Andrew Clapp, the first mayor of Portland. They have square stepped bases and ground decorations on the very graceful balloon-shaped oil fonts. Another tall lamp with a similar oil font, showing the long camphene burner and a many stepped base, belonged to Henry Wadsworth Longfellow.

The so-called "White House" of the Confederacy, once the home of Jefferson Davis, yielded a lamp of the coveted canary yellow glass. Still another historic lamp came from the home of General Joseph Hooker, "Fighting Joe." This has a square base, a rather short urn-shaped font with a cut design and a very much elongated stem. A somewhat smaller lamp with a round base and paneled font was found in the Confederate Hospital at Vicksburg, Mississippi, after the surrender of the city. A pair of stately opaque bridal lamps would seem to have happier associations. A rather rare variant of this class of lamps is the one showing a blown glass globe inserted, as it were, in the stem, between the base and the oil font.

Up to this time whale oil had been the commonly used illuminant. The discovery of petroleum about 1859, leading to the manufacture of kerosene, sounded the death knell of the older oil whose use had persisted despite the steadily increasing popularity of the Argand burner. In-

deed, within twenty-five years at least one store in western Massachusetts continued to carry whale oil, because
an old and honored customer steadfastly refused to use
any other!

Working on the Argand burner, Benjamin Thompson,
better known as Count Rumford, though he was a native-
born American, made several improvements and secured
a better light both by the use of a multiple burner and by
changes in the outward form, developing the type that
has the lamp proper supported by a slender arm which
extends at right angles to the oil reservoir. This was
known as the astral lamp, though later the name came to
be loosely applied to a much larger class of lamps.

These first astral lamps were usually made of bronze,
with ground glass globes, plain or etched, and were designed especially for the mantel, a complete set consisting of a two-branched piece for the center and a single
arm lamp for either end. Hung with well-cut prisms
many of them were very handsome, having a dignity and
solidity wholly lacking in the earlier lamps. Any suggestion of heaviness, however, is obviated by the use of
the prisms, those gleaming, sparkling pendants which
catch the sunlight and thereby release a joyous troop of
rainbow fairies to dance about the room in frocks of red
and yellow and violet.

The invention and perfection of the modern electric

lamp has not only turned night into day, in city, camp and country, but has incidentally brought back to us our beautiful Sandwich lamps, fit holders for the clear, clean light of the twentieth century.

CANDLES AND CANDLESTICKS

GLASS CANDLESTICKS

CRYSTAL DOLPHIN CANDLESTICK, BLUE CANDLESTICK
WITH WHITE BASE, AND PETAL LAMP

## Chapter Fourteen

ONLY an old gray ginger jar with an untidy bunch of
gnarled and knubbly twigs threaded with tiny blue-gray
berries.  Yet, looking at it we feel the clean salt tang of
the east wind, we see a wild rose thicket close set against
a strip of shining sand, beyond, a line of silver foam,
and then, the sea!  Surely there is magic in the bayberry, for even though it be embodied in a candle it still
suggests all manner of delightful things.  It brings us
a breath of the moors, glimpses of purple and gold in
asters and golden rod, masses of low-growing scrubby
bushes thick with silvery waxen berries or nuts.  And
then we see merry groups of young folk trooping home
laden with those same berries.  We see the colonial
kitchen, its blazing fire beneath the stout crane, the big
black kettles with the melting wax, the candle rods with
their suspended wicks, the careful housewife keeping her
wax at just the right temperature for "dipping," the finished candle of exquisite cool green.  All this and more
we see in that small bunch of berries.  Like many another bit of homely decoration it starts us off on a fascinating trail which carries us overseas and far afield.

Though candles cannot by any stretch of the imagination be classed as glass, yet they are so closely related to candlesticks that it is impossible to think of one without thinking of the other, and the bayberry candle is so inalienably attached to the glass candlestick that a little digression seems inevitable at this point.

In the earliest days of American housekeeping, when the colonists had "moved in," so to speak, but weren't settled, candles were both scarce and costly. The commonly used light was candlewood, slivers of pitch pine cut in convenient lengths and thrust into the cracks of the fireplace or into rude holders. These made a brilliant light and were in keeping with the simple furnishings of the primitive homes. To be sure, they smoked more or less and dripped, but they were inexpensive and easily available, to be had for the cutting, so that they remained in use long after candles came. Indeed, the pine torch may still be used in some of the outlying districts of the south.

After the candlewood, came rushlights, bundles of rushes or reeds tied together, saturated with grease, and burned. The old rushlight holders are interesting reminders of the days of our forefathers, crude iron devices like tongs which held the rushes firm. They were commonly provided with an arm which had a candle socket, thus serving two purposes.

# Candles and Candlesticks

Candlesticks as we know them were extremely rare in these days, though there were a few imported. One of these, known as the "Endicott Candlestick," was brought over by Governor Endicott when he came in 1628.

The first candles were, for the most part, held in wooden candle stands or beams. These consisted of a wooden bar provided with sockets, supported by an upright with heavy wooden base, and were made to hold several candles or only one. Some show two jointed arms with a socket at the end to hold the candle.

After these wooden beams came iron stands known variously as candlestands, torchères, and prickets; the latter having a sharp iron spike instead of a socket, to hold the candle. Some of the old torchères still have their snuffers and extinguishers hanging in place, for, unlike the modern candle, the old-fashioned "taller-dip" or even the molded candle, was not sufficient unto itself. Like the early lamp, it demanded frequent cleaning to insure a bright light. Otherwise, the wick became charred and produced a smoky flame. Everyday snuffers were made of iron, brass, or steel, but the dressy ones were of Sheffield plate or silver with tray to match. For some unknown reason the Sheffield candlesticks of to-day are still made with snuffers and extinguishers, though they are no longer necessary.

The extinguishers were simply metal caps for quenching the flame, thus avoiding the unpleasant odor which may come from the smoking wick. Mounted to long handles, they are still used in churches.

Even more necessary than the snuffers and extinguishers was the tinder box with its flint, steel, and bit of charred linen or "tinder," for without them there might be no light unless such was to be had from the blazing fire on the hearth. When this was available it was always an easier way to get it than from the soultrying flint and steel.

A less essential but more ornamental adjunct to the candle, though not so early, were the candle shades, or, as they were sometimes called, hurricane glasses. These were large shades or chimneys placed over the candle to protect it from drafts, and were commonly used in the south. Many of them were beautifully etched or engraved. Some interesting ones may be seen in Washington's home at Mt. Vernon. Placed over handsome candlesticks of silver or glass they were very decorative, enhancing the beauty of the candlestick, as well as steadying the flame.

Back in the days of home production, before machines did all our work for us, candles were made in two ways. The earlier process was known as dipping, and consisted of repeatedly dipping the suspended wicks into the melted fat or grease until they attained the requisite size. It demanded no inconsiderable skill, for the fat must be kept at just the right temperature, not sufficiently hot to melt the wax already on the wick, yet warm enough to insure a smooth surface; and the candle must be cooled after each dipping. An initial bath of saltpeter was said to make the candle burn more evenly and also to lessen the danger of "gutters," that distressing waste caused by the doubling over of the burning wick until it came in contact with the body of the candle, melting it away. Such a wick was known as a "candle robber." Despite the time and labor involved in this method a skillful worker might make two hundred candles in a day.

Eventually candle molds were introduced, groups of tin or pewter cylinders into which the heated grease was poured. These facilitated the work and produced a better or at least more symmetrical candle. The molds had from two to two dozen barrels, the twelve-barrel one being perhaps the best liked, though six and eight were not uncommon. The four, six and twelve were the most common in the tin molds. Besides these groups there were wooden stands which held twenty-four single molds. In the molded candle as in the dipped, the wicks were suspended over a rod placed across the top of the mold. These candles, therefore, always show a loop in the top.

Tallow, such a commonplace with us, was hard to come by in the early days, for there were practically no cattle, if one excepts the three historic cows imported from England in 1630. But the settlers, with the true pioneer spirit, made the most of what was at hand, and turned the fat of bear and deer to good account, supplementing it with the wax plundered from the wild bees. Bayberries, or, as they are sometimes happily called, candleberries, yielded a most satisfactory wax, though it required a whole quart of the little silver gray globes to produce one candle.

Life was a serious affair then, with not too many merry-makings. It is pleasant to think that the gathering of bayberries may have been the occasion of a family or a neighborhood picnic, when mother and the young folks would start off with baskets and lunch to make a day of it in the "blue October weather." Arrived home, the fragrant berries were stored in the attic to dry, perchance to await the coming of the candle maker, for as candles came more and more into general use, men went from house to house making a year's supply. It was the day of the journeyman, and his coming was eagerly looked forward to; for newspapers were unknown and the itinerant craftsman acted as a lively edition of the local sheet. News, gossip, and good stories were part of his stock in trade, and he was ever a welcome visitor.

# Candles and Candlesticks

Perhaps the chief charm of the bayberry is its delicate aromatic odor, a fugitive fragrance, not to be had from the burning candle. It is only when the light is blown out that one gets it, surely the most elusive incense in the world. We are told that it was no uncommon thing, if one had visitors, to extinguish the candle that the fragrance might be released. But the "bayberry dip" had other more practical virtues, in that it was not greasy and did not soften in warm weather, a sturdy quality indeed.

As whaling increased it was found that the fatty substance in the head of the sperm whale made excellent candles, giving a far better light than the more commonly used tallow candles.

The sconce was probably one of the early types of candlestick. They were of tin, pewter, brass, and copper, and ranged from the simple wall piece of metal with no attempt at decoration to those showing reflectors of cut glass and silver. Those of cut glass are, of course, by far the most brilliant and also very rare. Some have a perfectly plain piece of looking glass fitted together in such a way as to intensify the light tremendously. Sometimes molded glass was quicksilvered or melted pewter was poured over the cut glass. In all these divers ways did these craftsmen endeavor to make the most of their light.

[ 165 ]

# American Glass

A pair of candlesticks which has both historic and individual interest are those given by Benjamin Franklin to the fair Dorothy Quincy on the occasion of her marriage to John Hancock, Revolutionary hero and man of affairs. These candlesticks have a rubber-like substance on the bottom which makes it possible to fasten them to the wall or the mirror by suction. A joint below the candle socket permits of bending the socket at right angles to the stem. Thus they may be used either upright on the dressing table or as side lights on the mirror, a double use which would be much appreciated in the days when there were no brilliant side lights to aid the young beauties in making their elaborate toilets.

While candlesticks of silver or Sheffield plate have a certain stately dignity, a well designed glass candlestick has a sparkle and character all its own. Some very interesting and beautiful ones were made by the Sandwich Glass Company, though their output in this line did not at all equal that of lamps. The Dolphin is perhaps their most famous pattern, and he who has inherited a pair of Dolphin candlesticks in canary yellow is fortunate indeed, though these have not the depth and richness of those made in deep wine red or dazzling blue. A pair of wine colored candlesticks are beautiful enough to put upon an altar.

Many of the candlesticks show bases similar to those of

the lamps and like these latter there are often different tops combined with one style of base. These are stepped, octagonal, square, round and fluted. Among the tops the tulip is probably the best known, though there are flat and saucer-shaped tops.

A particularly attractive Sandwich candlestick is of opalescent glass, the slight graceful figure of a woman bearing the candle socket on her head. Much more elaborate is a pair which show both molding and cutting, the flaring tops being cut in sharp points, the whole decorated with cut prisms. The prisms give an air of elegance not always associated with candlesticks, though it is very marked in the candelabra, those dignified aristocrats of the candle world, with their tinkling, swinging prisms radiating light and color. Often candlesticks were made in pairs, sometimes with an accompanying squat little holder for lamplighters, those slender twists of paper which used always to be kept on hand, and the making of which beguiled many an idle moment or helped to pass a rainy day. The mercury-blown pieces were frequently decorated with bunches of flowers in gay colors, and many a mantel shelf boasted its glittering candlestick on either end with the small quaint holder in the center.

MISCELLANEOUS GLASS

## Chapter Fifteen

No outline of the glass industry as carried on in our country would be complete without mention of the miscellaneous pieces. This does not mean the worthless odds and ends looked over in the semi-annual cleaning days, but includes many an exquisite bit of great interest to collectors; single pieces, picked up here and there, so interesting in color and shape that one delights to gather them into groupings.

Among these odd bits are perfume bottles, pieces of jewelry, paper weights, door knobs, and a hundred and one other articles that have come into existence since the making of glass was started in this country.

Many of these pieces are the result of individual initiative, and for this reason are even more interesting than the standardized articles made in quantity by the various glass manufacturers. It was a common practice in the old glass houses to allow the workers to use up the metal that was left over after the regular work for the day or the week was completed. Sometimes odds and ends of metal were cleared out of the pots and thrown together in one pot, which was kept for this purpose, and the workmen were at liberty to use it as they liked.

# American Glass

No doubt much of the table glass that we are treasuring at present was made in this way, as mentioned in the chapter on Table Glass; and it is certain that many of the little novelties that ornament our cabinets and writing desks owe their existence to this state of affairs. Some of them were made and sold for small sums by ambitious workers who wanted to earn a little money "on the side;" some were made for family use in the worker's own home; and some no doubt came into being merely through the urge to create that animates every one who has the smallest gift in any of the arts.

A glass blower should and usually does possess some degree of artistic ability, and this was even more true in the early days than it is now, when there are so many mechanical aids for the worker to depend upon. It is easy to picture a blower in one of those old time glass houses gathering a small parison of blue or amber metal on his blowpipe and turning it into a little hat or a funny toy animal to delight his small daughter; and although quantities of such oddments were made as part of the regular output of many factories, there is little doubt that some of the rarest specimens owe their rarity to the fact that they were made in small quantities, perhaps only a single one of a kind, by some worker who was doing it "on his own," after his day's work was finished. No doubt, too, some of the strange inequalities and lopsidednesses that so delight our hearts at present are due to this practice, as are the unexpected flecks of red in a green salt cellar or a curiously mottled pitcher, the result of throwing together remnants of metal cleared from several pots.

Any one whose memory goes back for thirty years or more can probably remember some old fashioned "parlor" where glass filled a prominent part in the decoration of the room. Perhaps on the mantel there was a pair of vases of brilliant silvery glass, or a pair of candlesticks of similar material. Such vases and candlesticks were made by mixing silver with the molten glass. It is said that handfuls of silver dollars were added to at least one batch, and the result was a silvery glass of wonderfully mellow tone. It was an expensive process, however, and quicksilver was generally substituted, resulting in what is known as mercury-blown glass. This was used for door knobs, candlesticks, vases, and similar articles. Door knobs of the real silver glass may still be seen in the house which Deming Jarves built for his son, affording an opportunity to compare the effect of the genuine metal with that of the cheaper substitute.

Glass knobs for furniture were made in many designs and colors. In an old advertisement which appeared in the *American Daily Advertiser*, in Philadelphia, March 4, 1830, the advertiser, M. Nisbit, offered glass commode knobs "in superior double flint glass, plain, fluted, fine twisted, coarse twisted, molded and sunflower," also "the same as the above of the following colors, viz., Deep Blue, Turquoise, Opal, Pearl, Agate."

These knobs were from the Jersey Glass Company, and, Mr. Nisbit declared, "in point of shape and quality of glass, not surpassed by any in the country; prices very low." Further on, the advertisement offered to receive orders for "Cut Glass Knobs of any pattern required," and stated that there was on hand "an invoice of extra rich Cut Glass Knobs and a few Signal Lanterns."

There were other knobs and rosettes, very ornate and often really beautiful, made sometimes in clear glass but more often in opal glass. These were screwed into the wall and used too for the hanging of pictures or mirrors, or to hold back curtains. Great quantities were made at Sandwich about 1840, and have been reproduced in even larger quantities of recent years. Some of these reproductions are honestly sold as reproductions, while others have been offered to the unsuspecting collector as genuine antiques.

This question of reproductions and imitations is one that ought to be clearly differentiated. Reproductions have always been made and will always be made as long as the world lasts. Stiegel and Wistar reproduced designs that had been worked out by the English and Dutch

PITCHER OF AMBERINA ON WHICH
THE FIGURES SHOW PLAINLY

(Courtesy of the Toledo Museum of Art)

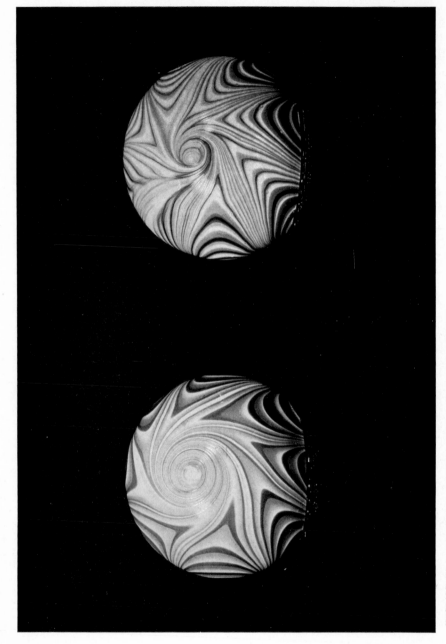

WISTABBERG WITCH BALLS, TWENTY INCHES IN CIRCUMFERENCE

A BLUSH APPLE, MADE IN SANDWICH

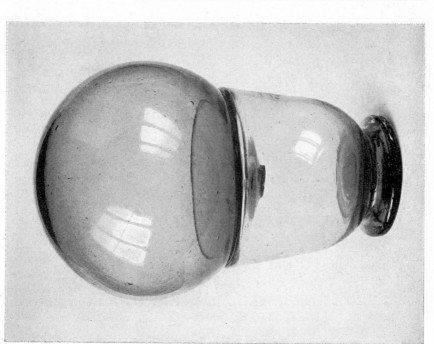

LATE EIGHTEENTH CENTURY WISTARBERG BOWL
WITH BALL COVER

CLEAR AND OPAQUE GLASS BUREAU KNOBS MADE AT SANDWICH, MASS.

and German glass houses, which in turn reproduced from older craftsmen, adding notes of originality and making ware that was distinctly their own, and offered as their own. These we may call honest reproductions. If they had sold them as English or German glass they would properly be called imitations; and indeed it was one of Stiegel's continual grievances that some of the merchants who sold his goods did represent them as importations because, they said, people would not buy glass of native manufacture.

In the chapter on Table Glass mention was made of glass balls, used as covers for bowls and pitchers. They were made in all sorts of colors and combinations of colors, as well as in a wide range of sizes; and in addition to their service as covers they found other ways of making themselves both useful and decorative.

Sometimes they were provided with a hole in the bottom. In this case they were called "Witch Balls," and were placed on the end of a stick which was set upon the window sill to drive away witches. Again, they were hung from the rafters to perform the same service.

It is said that they were sometimes enclosed in a mesh of cord and fastened by fishermen to the edges of their nets where they bobbed up and down and notified the anxious watchers when their nets were full.

Sometimes they were provided with a metal stand and

allowed to be merely a thing of beauty, adding a note of color to a dark corner of the room, a use to which they are often put in these modern days.

There is a type of glass seldom seen among the collections of to-day. It is known as Amberina. This was originated by William L. Libbey during the period when he was Superintendent of the New England Glass Works, at East Cambridge. So rare has this glass become that one gloats over every fine specimen picked up at auction or discovered in an antique shop or farmhouse. Amberina is well worth hunting for, as it displays a beautiful ruby tint shading into straw, a hue caused by the adding of gold to the batch.

A number of pieces are owned by William S. Walbridge of Toledo, Ohio. One of the most interesting, as a picture of the fashions of fifty years ago, is a lemonade pitcher, commonly called a tankard. It is decorated with bands of tennis racquets at top and bottom, and between these bands figures of ladies in the garb of 1880 or thereabouts are shown playing tennis on a grass court.

One of the most extraordinary feats of glass manipulation on record resulted when Georgia Cayvan, the actress, ordered during the Libbey exhibition at the Chicago World's Fair, in 1893, a dress made entirely of spun glass. This was so beautiful that it attracted the attention of the Infanta Eulalia of Spain, for whom a similar gown was manufactured. This second dress is now preserved in the Deutsche Museum at Munich.

The spun glass used in these garments was so finely drawn that the threads have the appearance and suppleness of the finest silk, and the fabric gives the effect of a very beautiful gleaming silken textile. A jacket and four-in-hand scarf made in the same way are now hanging in the office of the Owens Bottle Company in Toledo.

However, pieces such as these are interesting principally as examples of the wonders that can be accomplished by this versatile material, in the hands of a skilled manipulator, and do not possess the same attraction for the collector as articles that he may some day hope to own. Fortunately the list of such things is long and includes so great a variety in color, shape and size that even now, when the field has been very thoroughly combed, there is opportunity for every one to secure some things of charm and interest.

Among the novelties that add variety to a miscellaneous collection of old glass are novelties in the form of darners, rolling pins, small hats designed for the holding of tapers, door stops in the form of turtles, dogs, cats, and other varieties of fauna, bellows in blue glass with white beaded edges, and emerald green paper weights in the shape of pineapples. Glass imitations of candy canes, finished in opaque white, with red, green and blue stripes, to be hung by ribbons on the wall, were a popular feature of early interior decoration; and specimens are still to be found occasionally by those who are interested in the old and quaint.

The factory at Millville, New Jersey, made a great variety of novelties, including chains of glass, glass flowers, paper weights, and balls.

Of no less interest but usually of more intrinsic beauty, were the toilet cases, some of them finished with bronze casing and portraying woodland scenes and similar pictures etched on the glass. Some beautiful toilet bottles of deep blue glass with gilt leaf decoration were made by Stiegel, and other bottles intended for the same use were turned out in quantities by all the manufacturers.

Inkstands were another favorite product, and these are to be found in various grades and shapes, from the beautiful millefiori ones to heavy and rather crude ones in three mold design but in coarse brown or green glass.

Millefiori, or "glass of a thousand flowers," as the literal translation of the Italian phrase would be, deserves more than a passing notice. It was made in this country both in the original form perfected by the Venetians and in adaptations of various kinds.

The true millefiori is an ancient form of glass work, going back to Rome and perhaps to Egypt. It was revived and very highly developed in Venice in the twelfth century and again in the nineteenth; and between 1850 and 1870 it enjoyed a great vogue in this country.

The true millefiori is made by arranging rods of glass of various colors so that their ends made a design, such as a bouquet of flowers with green leaves, or a single blossom with petals, pistils and stamens represented each by a rod of appropriate color. These rods are fused together by heat and are then drawn out to any desired length, the design remaining the same in form but growing smaller as the rod becomes longer.

It is easily seen that wherever this rod, made by the fusing together of the smaller rods, is sliced through, the same design will be presented as on the end. If it is sliced diagonally the design will be slightly different in effect, and considerable variety can be secured by changing the angle of the cuts.

A slice of this rod, or several slices, may be cut off and covered with a bubble of plastic glass which is shaped in any desired form and allowed to harden with the design inside. When the surface of the clear glass is convex, as in the case of most paper weights, the design is magnified by the convexity and presents a different appearance from different angles of vision.

This idea was used in an infinite number of combinations and in articles of various sorts, such as inkstands, bottle stoppers, sweetmeat jars, perfume bottles, brooches and other bits of jewelry, door knobs, letter seals, vases and incense burners; and a collection of millefiori can combine in a small space more varied and fascinating shapes and colors than any other type of glass. The shelf of a cabinet or the top of a table holding a dozen of these gay little pieces is a constant joy when the sun strikes it and a bit of cheering colorful life on a cloudy day.

# THE STORY OF GLASS

## Chapter Sixteen

THE collector may collect from varied motives. Some love old things merely because they are old; others care to have only articles that are beautiful, whether old or new; and still others are interested in anything, beautiful or ugly, which forms a link in the history of an industry, a nation, or the human race. The character of a collection depends upon the motive that actuates the collector. Sometimes, as he learns more about the subject, he may broaden or restrict the scope of the collection. Whatever basis of glass selection you may choose you will be able to collect more efficiently and to enjoy your collection more intelligently if you know something more than the surface facts about it.

The word "glass" is applied to such a variety of substances that it is all but impossible to define it satisfactorily without giving a whole volume to the subject. However, this is not a technical treatise so I am not going to attempt anything in the nature of a scientific analysis. Walter Rosenhain, in his book "Glass Manufacture," suggests as a succinct description of glass the phrase "A congealed liquid," and this at least has the value of painting a vivid mind-picture of the clear, hard, brittle material that we generally think of as glass. As a matter of fact there are all sorts of things that look quite unlike this, but that are entitled to the name.

There is for instance a natural glass, found in the vicinity of volcanoes, and known as obsidian. This is generally dark in color and is not the sort of thing that comes to mind when we use the word "glass." Nevertheless it is a true glass.

The one essential thing that, according to the technically trained, makes glass different from other substances which look much like it, such as ice or rock crystal, is that these have a crystalline structure and glass is "vitreous" or "amorphous" in its makeup. This amorphous structure accounts for its well known tendency to fly into pieces when it is dropped or struck.

If a cake of ice is pierced with a sharp implement, in the right direction, it can be split pretty accurately along a predetermined line. That is because its molecules are grouped in definite crystals which separate from one another under force. In glass, so far as any one can discover, there is no geometrical arrangement of molecules, and when the same experiment that was tried on the ice is tried with a piece of glass, it does not matter where or how the force is applied, the glass will break with equal ease in any or all directions and no one can foresee the course of the fracture. If it is scratched with a diamond or seared along a line with a red hot poker it can usually (though not invariably) be broken where the break is wanted, but so far as the internal structure of the material is concerned there is no "grain" in glass that determines the course of a crack or break.

In the process of manufacture, too, its erratic behavior causes a good deal of trouble to its makers, though more in former times than at present. Modern laboratory methods have taken away some of the uncertainty that used to make glass manufacture a hazardous though fascinating enterprise. But with all the aids of modern invention and scientific knowledge, it is still a strange, capricious substance, of great potential beauty and utility, but with limitations beyond which the skill of man has not yet been able to force it.

Fire is the only element to which it yields completely. Water and air may affect it to some extent, through long periods of time—the amount of their influence depending largely upon the proportions in which the ingredients were mixed—but heat of great intensity is the only master to which it gives a ready obedience. Under the influence of fire it is plastic, so that man can bend and shape it to his uses, but once the heat is removed and the fluid congealed, no force can affect its shape except by destroying it. However, if it is subjected again to the fire it will again become plastic, and this can be repeated over and over with only one danger. If it is heated too often, or kept at a certain temperature for too long a time, it loses its vitreous structure and becomes crystalline; and then its beauty and its strength are destroyed.

In the story told by Pliny, and mentioned at the beginning of the book, the basic ingredients of glass were mentioned—silica, which was present in the sand of the beach; soda, which supplied the essential alkali; and ashes of seaweed which acted as a flux and helped in the dissolving and mingling of the sand and soda; so if the necessary heat had only been present the sailors might really have been the accidental discoverers of this useful material.

The essential ingredients of glass have just been mentioned—silica and an alkali. As a matter of fact the thing is not as simple as this. In all manufactured glass there are at least three, and often more than three, ingredients, some of them present as accidents and some of them by design. The color of early bottles, for instance, which has given us the term "bottle green," was not due to intent on the part of the maker but to the fact that the bottles were made of the cheapest possible ingredients, and that the manufacturer did not think it was worth while or did not have facilities to rid them of the metallic oxides and other impurities that gave the glass its color.

Silica is a mineral that occurs in many combinations

all over the world, and the form as well as the proportion in which it is used has a bearing upon the kind of glass produced. It is present in rock crystal, and in ancient times it was the aim of glass makers to produce a glass as white and clear as pure crystal. Indeed an early name for transparent, colorless glass was crystal glass, and the term is still in use to-day.

The form in which silica is found most commonly is sand. The mouth of the river Belus, mentioned in Pliny's story, was a famous source of glass sand in ancient times, and tradition says that Venice in the heyday of her supremacy as a glass producing community used to send to this far off shore for supplies. Not all sand is good glass sand, however, and even among the sands that can be used for making glass some are better than others for certain varieties. For instance, sand that is quite good enough for rough bottles may not do at all for fine tableware, or may require so much refining that it would not pay to use it.

Generally speaking, the more silica glass contains, in proportion to its other ingredients, the harder the glass is; though sometimes this hardness is counteracted by one of the other ingredients. Lead, for example, tends to soften glass, as well as to add to its luster—characteristics that had their bearing upon the development of pressed glass, which is mentioned in other parts of the book.

Any attempt to give formulas for different kinds of glass would be outside of the scope of this volume, but the person who is setting out to be a glass collector should bear in mind that different kinds of glass differ from one another in the ingredients used as well as in the shape of the article or the processes of blowing, pressing, casting, rolling, polishing, and decorating that give form and finish to the object; whether it be a salt cellar, a plate glass window or the lens for an eyeglass. Some of these differences are mentioned wherever they help to make clear the qualities to be looked for in a special kind of glass or the origin and meaning of the terms used in speaking about it.

Even more important than a knowledge of the ingredients used, is some acquaintance with the processes by which glass is made, shaped and finished; and any one who has an opportunity to visit a glass factory will find it an interesting and enlightening experience. Probably to the uninitiated there is more fascination in watching hand processes, which are still employed in the making of fine glassware, than in the necessarily more mechanical methods used where great quantities of articles are turned out. Nevertheless, these modern machines, which do things that a few years ago would have been considered impossible, have a magnificence of their own.

# The Story of Glass

In his book "American Bottles," William S. Walbridge quotes from an article published in London *Truth* of December 11, 1907, written by a man who had seen a bottle making machine in operation in Germany:

"Certainly," this Englishman wrote, "of all the evil looking machinery I have seen—and I have been privileged to see a good deal in my time—I have never seen any which gives so exactly the appearance of an angry —even malignant—idol.

"I dare swear that if Arminius or any other of the old-time gods of the Ahr Valley were to have seen it, they would have prostrated themselves before it as a worthy supplanter of their former gods and within an hour or so would have been offering human sacrifices, too, in its honor.

. . . . . .

"I have neither the inclination nor the capacity to describe it in detail—suffice to say that it performs the whole operation of bottle-making from the beginning to end, without once calling for human intervention. It even dips the molten glass out of the furnace with one pair of steel hands, with them crams it into the molds, which may well represent its maw, retreats with it from the furnace as might a dog that has snatched a bone; molds, blows it and tempers it, and who knows what besides, finally delivering the finished bottle to its expectant attendant as though, having sucked the warm marrow from the bone, it was content to resign the empty covering to others."

However, it was a long road from ancient Egypt to this glass eating monster, and most of the history of glass making revolves around operations that range from the small crucibles in which the early craftsmen probably melted their raw materials to pots and furnaces of gradually increasing size but of the same general structure.

The pots that were used by the glass makers of Murano in the middle ages might be considered typical containers for molten glass, and their early tools as the typical tools of the industry. Throughout the centuries up to the time when this age of machinery developed such fiery monsters as the one just described, the changes were changes in details only—enlarging of the pots, perfecting of the furnaces, alterations in the hand tools from time to time—but the methods of blowing glass are essentially the same as they were five thousand years ago, and even the pressing of glass, which we have been led to think of as a new thing, was, according to Mr. Biser, practiced in the days when Thebes was one of the great cities of the world.

The essential requirements for glass making, next to the ingredients themselves, are some sort of a pot in which to melt the raw materials, some sort of fuel to give the necessary heat, some sort of a furnace to concentrate this heat and make it effective, and tools to take out the plastic glass or "metal" and form it into the desired shape.

SANDWICH GLASS TURTLE DOOR STOP

A JAR, TWIN BOTTLE, COMPOTE, AND BALL-SHAPED
JAR COVER FROM STODDARD, N. H.

SANDWICH LAMP, PETAL DESIGN, ON A MARBLE STAND.
TWO RARE AMBER COLORED CANDLESTICKS

# The Story of Glass

In the early days, when transportation was difficult, a supply of fire clay and an abundance of fuel often determined the location of a glass factory. In England at one time it was a common practice to abandon a glass house as the timber in the locality was burned up and build a new one where conditions were more favorable. As a result the forests of England were seriously threatened with extermination and laws were passed prohibiting the use of wood as fuel in the making of glass. Even very recently in this country, with all the facilities of transportation available, the practice of choosing a site for a glass house because of accessible fuel had not been abandoned. Mr. Walbridge records that in 1909 "a site was purchased near Fairmont, West Virginia, contiguous to the gas and coal fields."

The typical glass melting pot is made of fire clay, which glass makers from the earliest time have found to be the best material, though in the great manufactories of to-day iron tanks are often used. The making of the pot is an industry by itself, requiring a knowledge of the right kind of clay and the best methods of digging, preparing and handling it. In the old days the work was done entirely by hand and the building of a pot meant a long and anxious period for the maker.

The first step in the making of a typical pot is the digging and grinding of the virgin clay until it forms a powder of the required fineness, which is then mixed with a certain amount of clay that has been burned. Sometimes old pots are ground up; sometimes fresh clay is burned especially for the purpose. The reason for using this burned clay with the fresh is to help prevent the development of cracks while the pots are drying out. Also, since this clay has already been burned, and has in consequence lost the natural moisture that is present in fresh clay, there is less contraction during the period of drying that must follow than there would be if virgin clay alone were used.

After the fresh clay and the burned clay are thoroughly mixed they are "wet up" with water until the mass forms a stiff dough, which is vigorously kneaded. In old times this kneading was done with bare feet, treading out the mass until it had reached a satisfactory consistency. After the kneading it is stored for a considerable time, in its damp condition. This storing brings out the full toughness and plasticity of the clay. The next step is to form it into rolls, which are built up, one on top of the other. The work must be done gradually and all cracks smoothed out, and each day the growing pot must be left to dry overnight.

Some pots are open, much in shape like an ordinary pail. Others are covered with a dome shaped roof, having an opening on one side near the top, so that they present much the appearance of a medieval helmet with the visor open.

After the pot is completed, a matter of several weeks, it is allowed to dry. This drying process may take several months, and when the pot is ready to be taken into use it appears to the uninitiated to be literally "dry as a bone." As a matter of fact, however, there is still moisture chemically present in the innermost structure of the substance. In order to get rid of this before putting the pot into the furnace for use in holding the "metal," it has to be burned in a kiln, where it is gradually heated until it is red hot. Then it is removed to the furnace, which has also been heated to a high temperature, and is ready for the first "batch."

Into this red hot cavity the raw materials are fed, or "charged," and the process of "fusing" begins. When the melting and mingling have been completed, and the impurities have gone off in gases or have been skimmed from the molten mass, it is allowed to cool off until it reaches a temperature where it is ready for blowing. In this condition it is no longer liquid but viscous, so that it can be "gathered" up on the blow pipe and formed into a soft ball or egg-shaped mass.

The work of blowing centers around what is known as a "chair," a stout bench on which the worker can sit or stand, with long arms on which he can roll the blowpipe or the "pontil" while shaping the article. Each chair in a typical glass house has its own crew or "shop," consisting usually of three people, the gatherer, the blower and the man who handles the pontil.

The blowpipe is a hollow tube from four to six feet long, with a wooden mouthpiece and section for holding it at one end. The other end has an expanded lip. The size of the pipe and the size and shape of the expanded end are varied to take care of different kinds of glass blowing.

The gatherer inserts the heated end of the blowpipe into the pot and skillfully twists it until it is covered with a lump of the required size. For large objects it is sometimes necessary to withdraw the pipe and plunge it in again several times, each time gathering an additional layer of the viscous mass until the whole is of the desired size.

Then the gathering or "parison" is rolled on the "marver," a table which takes its name from the fact that it was originally made of marble. When the glass is shaped into a compact ball or ellipse, the blower, putting his mouth to the other end of the long pipe, begins to blow just as a child blows soap bubbles, and with much the same result. As he blows he manipulates the blowpipe, now swinging it from side to side, now rotating it rapidly. Sometimes he stands on the "chair" and lets the pipe hang down, at others he raises it into the air.

The process of blowing is one that requires a high degree of skill, and in order to produce beautiful articles by what is known as the "offhand" method of blowing, a blower must possess considerable artistic ability as well.

When the bubble has reached the required size and shape and thickness, or rather thinness, the pontil man attaches to his rod a small lump of the viscous glass or metal, and with this he affixes the end of the pontil rod or "punty" to a point directly opposite that at which the bubble is fastened to the blowpipe; so that it is held between two long rods, one hollow and the other solid, with a man holding each rod.

The article is now separated from the blowpipe by one means or another, according to the requirements of the occasion, but is left attached to the pontil iron while the final form is given to the article. This is done by means of various tools and devices, prominent among them being the "pucellas," a pair of blunt shears or tongs, used for shaping but not for cutting, and shears very much like the ordinary shears of household use, which are employed in cutting the plastic material. Traces of the pontil iron and of the shears are marks that help to identify old pieces as genuine, though as these marks can of course be made on modern imitations they cannot be accepted as infallible proof of antiquity.

When the piece has been finished, so far as its shaping is concerned, it is ready for the annealing oven, where it is first heated to a temperature almost but not quite high enough to melt it, and is then gradually cooled off. This annealing is necessary to prevent the article from cooling too suddenly on the surface while the molecules of the inner portions are still in a state of activity from the heat; because this would result in the piece flying to bits the first time it was exposed to any shock, even a very mild blow or scratch.

After the annealing it is ready for any external finishing that is to be applied, such as etching or cutting. Between blown glass of the offhand variety just described, and pressed glass, about which more will be said farther on, there is a process that partakes a little of each, known as glass blown in a mold. In this method of glass working, after the blower has made a small bubble on the end of his pipe, he inserts it into a mold, which has been cut or cast so that its inner surface forms a pattern of the shape and size desired for the outer surface of the finished object. As the blowing is continued the plastic glass is forced out into all the cavities of the mold. Since the bubble of glass is usually fairly thin, the result of the blowing is that the inner surface of the glass follows the same outline as the outer surface. That is, for each protuberance of any size on the outer surface, there is a corresponding depression on the inside, and vice versa.

Occasionally one sees mold-blown glass which does not have this unevenness on the inner surface, even when the outer surface has a pronounced pattern. This may be due to the fact that the metal was less hot than it usually is when blown, or it may be due to the fact that more glass was used, so that the walls are thicker and therefore less yielding to the breath than if they were more fragile.

In articles where the top is larger than any other part, such as a plain bowl, the mold can be made in one piece. Where the top is smaller than some other part, as in the case of a bottle, although the article might be blown perfectly within a one-piece mold, it is easily seen that it would be impossible to take the hardened article out. Therefore, molds are made in two or more pieces, hinged together, so that they can be opened to take out the finished article. Sometimes the sections open vertically, sometimes horizontally, according to the requirements of the shape. The sections, of course, must be very carefully fitted together and must be closed very tightly in order to prevent a seam or fin of glass from squeezing out through the fissures. As a matter of fact, glass blown in a mold is very likely to have such seams, especially when the molds are old.

Moreover, when hot glass comes into contact with a relatively cold mold the result is almost inevitable that the surface of the glass is roughened or crinkled more or less. Various methods are used to remedy this, such as dressing the molds with slippery substances and rotating the blowpipe during the process of blowing, so that the surface of the glass is smoothed or polished by rubbing against the mold. This second method can be used only where the mold is entirely plain and of a circular or elliptical shape. Where there is a raised or sunken pattern, or where the shape of the article is irregular, this tendency to roughness as well as the likelihood of seams or fins of glass is often taken into account in cutting the mold, and the design made so that the roughnesses will be concealed or will form part of the pattern.

In addition, a finish known as fire polish is often given to glass blown in a mold, as well as to pressed glass. This is done by exposing the article to a heat intense enough to melt the surface of the glass slightly. The result of course is that the roughnesses are melted away and the glass hardens with a smooth, brilliant effect.

The old three mold glass which is so much in demand at present was made in this manner, with the molds divided into three parts. Hence the name.

Often in the offhand method of blowing, a condensed pattern is impressed upon the parison by pressing it into a small mold known as a pattern mold. This leaves the design on the surface in ridges, whorls, or whatever the pattern may be, and as the blowing is continued the pattern expands, keeping its general outlines but in extended or distended form. This produces an internal arrangement just the opposite of that which results when an article is blown in a full size or contact mold.

In the contact mold blown glass there is a hollow on the inside to correspond with each protuberance on the outside, and vice versa. In an expanded pattern mold piece there is a hollow on the inside corresponding to each hollow on the outside, and a protuberance on the inside corresponding to each protuberance on the outside. The reason for this is easy to understand. If the pattern mold, for instance, has left a series of cuts in the surface of the glass bubble, the material will be thinner at these lines than between them. When the air expands the bubble, these thin parts will naturally yield more easily than the thicker ribs between, and the result will be that there will be a series of thick cords of glass with thin sections between, in practically the same outline on the inside as on the outside.

For pressed glass the outer molds are formed in the same way as for glass blown in a contact mold; sometimes in one piece, sometimes in hinged sections. In addition, there is an inner mold or plunger which takes the place of the blower's breath (or, in these days, compressed air) and forces the plastic glass into the cavities of the outer mold.

The invention of this process is usually credited to a worker in the Sandwich Glass Works, but, as mentioned in the chapter on Sandwich glass, this claim was not made by Deming Jarves, the founder and head of the Sandwich works.

By the use of a plunger it is possible to force the plastic glass into every crevice, however fine. As a result, the molds for pressed glass can have deeper and more intricate cutting than for glass blown in a mold—that is, when the blowing is done by human agency. Modern methods of utilizing compressed air make possible many things that the breath of the blower could not accomplish.

In pressed glass the place where training and skill are most needed in the man who handles the metal is in estimating the amount needed for a given article. It is easy to see that if too little is put into the mold there will be unfinished places on the outside where the glass failed to touch the mold; while if there is too much, the plunger cannot go down properly without having the glass overflow and damage the edge or without doing harm to the mold.

When the inner surface of pressed hollow ware is larger at the top than at the bottom, the entire article can be pressed in one piece. Where the opening is smaller than some other part of the cavity, so that it would not be possible to pull the plunger out after the glass had hardened, articles are often made in two or more sections, afterward fused together with heat.

The silica for the glass used in Venice was often obtained from pebbles of the kind called crystal pebbles, which abounded in the vicinity of the city. These were ground to the desired size and used instead of sand in the melting pot. To this fact some ascribe the name "crystal" glass, and perhaps it owed its name to this as much as to the fact that it looked like the rock crystal found in nature.

Flint glass probably took its name from the fact that while experiments were being made to find out what English materials were usable in the making of glass, native pebbles, known as flints, were ground up, just as in the case of the Venetians crystal pebbles were used. However, these were used only long enough to give their name to the new kind of glass—a glass in which lead is one of the important ingredients—and glass containing lead is known as flint glass to this day.

Batch is the term used to designate the raw materials that are charged into the melting pot.

Metal is the name given to the molten substance when it is ready for blowing.

Pot metal, in the language of glass makers, means glass with color put into the batch, so that it permeates the metal. When a coating of one color is applied to an article of clear glass or of another color, the article is said to be flashed. Stained or painted glass is made by applying to a glass surface a design in a special kind of molten glass which is then burned or annealed so that it becomes really a part of the surface.

# GLASS AS DECORATION

## Chapter Seventeen

WITHIN the last few years glass collecting has become a fashion, and it is doubtful whether any other fashion can bring one more completely under its spell than addiction to this picturesque substance. It is so beautiful, even in quite crude forms, it can be used for so many purposes, both practical and artistic, it lends character and decorative value to every room in the house, and it has the charm that always attaches to the mysterious, to that which you can see and feel and enjoy but not quite understand. Because, when all is said and done, it is a substance about which little is known, and which arouses in the mind of any one with a spark of imagination the same wonder that old Dr. Johnson expressed two hundred years ago.

"Who," he queried, "when he first saw the sand and ashes by casual intenseness of heat melted into a metalline form, rugged with excrescences and clouded with impurities, would have imagined that in this shapeless mass lay concealed so many conveniences of life as would in time constitute a great part of the happiness of the world?"

[ 205 ]

# American Glass

One of the most attractive of the many attractive aspects of glass collecting is the opportunity it offers for combining utility with pure enjoyment of color and form. Old pieces are being taken out of the employment for which they were designed and raised to positions of greater honor. For instance, bowls, long ago made for dairy or kitchen, are now gracing our tables filled with blossoms that harmonize with the clear tints of their substance.

Other pieces, designed for utility but now used merely as ornaments, bring color into dull spots or combine with other articles in the room to make an effective group. If you have a piece of rose colored glass, for example, try setting it near a bit of copper and see how each intensifies the beauty of the other.

Glass, to be enjoyed to the fullest possible extent, should be clean and sparkling, especially when it depends for its beauty upon its transparency, as in clear flint or crystal. All that is necessary to keep it in this condition ordinarily is to wash it with warm soap suds and rinse in clear water, polishing it dry with a soft cloth. If a dish or bottle has a light sediment that will not wash off in this way, it may sometimes be removed by the use of fresh egg shells. Crush the shells and put them into the piece to be cleaned; cover them with water and allow them to stay for several hours. Then shake or mop the liquid and the crushed shells around the inside of the article and rinse with clear water.

When the sediment is too stubborn to yield to these mild measures, a solution of hydrochloric or muriatic acid may be poured into the article and allowed to remain until the crust is loosened. The glass should then be rinsed with clear water and dried and polished with a soft cloth.

Glass is not harmed by any of the substances ordinarily used in the household, and is not subject to injury from sunlight, except where, as sometimes happened, old glass had too much alkali mixed with the batch. In such a case exposure to sunlight will make clear glass take on a purplish tinge, as happened to the windows in Boston, mentioned in the chapter on Windows.

Aside from breakage, the worst enemy of glass is moisture, and valuable glass should never be stored in a damp cellar or left in any place where moisture can attack it. Long exposure to dampness sometimes produces very beautiful results, as in the bits of old glass often seen in museums, which owe their iridescent surface to this very factor; but those of us who have collections of glass that we want to keep clear and sparkling will do well to keep them in a dry place.

For collections that are too large or too valuable to be used, even occasionally, in the service of the table or as individual ornaments in the decoration of the home, special methods of displaying them may be devised so that they will form essential parts of the interior decoration. One of the most delightful effects is obtained by having shelves built against a window, where the changing light from without plays upon the pieces, making a constantly varied and enchanting picture.

Any shallow alcove, especially one in a corner, where the wall is curved at the back, is admirably adapted for the display of glass. This may be fitted with concealed lights, which can be turned on to throw just the desired glow from above and below when the natural light in the room is too subdued to bring out the beauty of the glass.

A background of ground glass makes an effective setting, but any surface of neutral tone, not too dark, will make a good background for a collection of glass.

Whatever the collection may be, whether large or small, confined to one specialized line or of miscellaneous interest, it possesses potentialities of endless delight. There is a fascination in trying to identify each piece; to learn who the maker was, if possible; to pick up bits of romantic history connected with the various owners who had it before it came into your possession. And, above all, there is the joy of having always at hand

[ 208 ]

things that are in substance and form beautiful and interesting, things from which no amount of familiarity can take the magic and the mystery that are a part of glass.

THE END